"Are you going to kill my mommy and me?" I heard my daughter ask in a voice that was weak, shaken, and more childlike than I'd heard in years. I breathed a sob of relief and inhaled a noseful of carpet fibers. *She's alive! Thank God!* I wanted to look at her, see her eyes, touch her face, and calm her fear. I ached to let her know with a single glance that we would be all right. But I didn't know if that was true.

The man holding me down wouldn't let me pick up my head. Beneath the pounding of my heart, I heard someone unrolling and ripping what sounded like tape.

"I'll do anything," I pleaded with the masked strangers, "but please don't hurt my daughter."

HELD HOSTAGE

THE TRUE STORY OF A
MOTHER AND DAUGHTER'S KIDNAPPING

MICHELLE RENEE

with *New York Times* bestselling author
ANDREA CAGAN

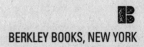

BERKLEY BOOKS, NEW YORK

THE BERKLEY PUBLISHING GROUP
Published by the Penguin Group
Penguin Group (USA) Inc.
375 Hudson Street, New York, New York 10014, USA

Penguin Group (Canada), 90 Eglinton Avenue East, Suite 700, Toronto, Ontario M4P 2Y3, Canada (a division of Pearson Penguin Canada Inc.)
Penguin Books Ltd., 80 Strand, London WC2R 0RL, England
Penguin Group Ireland, 25 St. Stephen's Green, Dublin 2, Ireland (a division of Penguin Books Ltd.)
Penguin Group (Australia), 250 Camberwell Road, Camberwell, Victoria 3124, Australia (a division of Pearson Australia Group Pty. Ltd.)
Penguin Books India Pvt. Ltd., 11 Community Centre, Panchsheel Park, New Delhi—110 017, India
Penguin Group (NZ), Cnr. Airborne and Rosedale Roads, Albany, Auckland 1310, New Zealand (a division of Pearson New Zealand Ltd.)
Penguin Books (South Africa) (Pty.) Ltd., 24 Sturdee Avenue, Rosebank, Johannesburg 2196, South Africa

Penguin Books Ltd., Registered Offices: 80 Strand, London WC2R 0RL, England

HELD HOSTAGE

Some names and identifying characteristics have been altered in an effort to safeguard the privacy of certain people.

A Berkley Book / published by arrangement with the author

PRINTING HISTORY
Berkley mass-market edition / December 2006

ISBN: 0-425-21301-3

BERKLEY®
Berkley Books are published by The Berkley Publishing Group,
a division of Penguin Group (USA) Inc.,
375 Hudson Street, New York, New York 10014.
BERKLEY is a registered trademark of Penguin Group (USA) Inc.
The "B" design is a trademark belonging to Penguin Group (USA) Inc.

PRINTED IN THE UNITED STATES OF AMERICA

10   9   8   7   6   5   4   3   2   1

For . . .
My strength, God
My hero, my brother Dave
My inspiration, violent crime victims
My greatest gift, my love, my joy, Breea

*I can be changed by what happens to me
but I refuse to be reduced by it.*

—MAYA ANGELOU

CONTENTS

PROLOGUE

I was nearly sixteen years old when I became an athlete, a runner. I'm not talking about the kind of athlete who wins marathons or Olympic gold medals. I was the kind of runner who climbed out of my second-story bedroom window and walked on tiptoes across the wooden beam over our covered patio, all the way to the edge. Once there, I stared at my feet, trembling and scared as hell. But there was no turning back. I had been beaten up and down by my father and was brokenhearted from hearing my mother weeping through paper-thin walls. I'd had enough.

I took a deep breath, mentally buried my childhood, and crouched into position, waiting for the crack of the starting gun that signaled the beginning of a lifelong dash. I drew my breath deeper, held it, soared into the air, and then landed on the soft green grass below, moist with midnight dew. I knew it immediately when I reached it—the taste of sweet freedom. I exhaled and ran as fast as my feet would carry me.

Twenty years later, a single mother and successful corporate ladder climber, I was still running. I was unaware, however, of the collision course that would soon force me into the pit of despair. A deep, dark hole where every shame-filled mistake, every glorious success, every face of every strange man for whom I took off my clothes, each burst of laughter, every tear I'd ever cried, and every other detail of my varied and colorful life, was alive and breathing, forcing me to confront myself.

At the age of thirty-five, the guns were not sounding off in my furiously pounding heart. If only it were that easy. This time, the icy barrels were firmly pressed against my temples because I was my tormentors' meal ticket, while the threat of my young daughter's demise ticked like a time bomb with every passing moment.

1. Desperate Strangers

BURNING vomit crept into my mouth. I swallowed. My hollow stomach was twisting and gnawing as I lay frozen in my bed, cradling her fragile frame in my arms. It was the middle of the night. I was drenched with cold perspiration and my heart raced with terror. I could smell the dank stench of them. I could hear their loathsome voices and I felt them crawling under my skin. I was afraid to close my eyes and I was afraid not to. I knew it didn't make any difference. They would always be there long after they were gone, penetrating the veils of my sleep, growling, "Shut up bitch, or we'll pistol-whip you in front of your kid."

NINE HOURS EARLIER

I glanced up at the large, round gold-rimmed clock on the bank wall. It read 5:45 PM. *Damn it!* I was going to be late . . . again. I pushed back from my desk, waved at Maria, my employee at the merchant window, and rushed out the double glass doors, heading for the parking lot.

The sun was setting on a cool Tuesday evening in Vista, California, a northern rural suburb of San Diego. I jumped into my 1994 red soft-top Jeep Wrangler, threw my leather briefcase into the backseat and deposited my cumbersome set of bank keys into the glove compartment. It was someone else's turn to lock up.

I stepped on the gas and sped down the country road until I came to a screeching halt in front of the small school-run daycare center. There she was, the most amazing person in my life, my seven-year-old daughter Breea, her bouncing blonde curls dancing around her soft pale face.

"How was your day, sweetie?" I asked as she hopped into the copilot seat.

"Can we have pizza for supper? Please?" she asked, clapping her hands as if I'd already agreed. It was hard to say no to Breea.

AFTER a quick stop at the local Super Saver, we pulled up in front of our cabin-style house on the hill. As always, my chocolate Lab I'd rescued from wandering the streets and my roommate's large black German shepherd, a gentle giant, ran up to greet us. That was when I noticed a fat Rottweiler I'd never seen before, panting and drooling. Where did he come from? I wondered. Not that the occasional stray was rare in our rural community. I looked him over, noticing that the dirty, frayed nylon cord tied around his neck and dragging on the ground was much too tight. He was pacing anxiously. He must have *just* gotten away, I thought to myself and briefly looked around for some sign of an owner.

I felt a familiar sense of the day's stress sloughing off like old skin. I closed my eyes and inhaled the cool evening air. When I reached into the Jeep and grabbed the thin plastic grocery bag from the backseat with one hand, it tore open. Cans and bottles spilled out onto the gravel driveway. *Shit!* I muttered to myself. I teetered on four-inch heels, maneuvering my ankle-length skirt while I chased a couple of rolling olive cans and tomato sauce to the nearby bushes. I bent over and then stopped in my position to listen to the sound of leaves being crushed and twigs breaking.

"Shhhhhh." I gestured to Breea. Our dogs weren't barking. Must have been a small animal like a squirrel or the stray dog. I gathered the rest of the scattered groceries and made my way into the house.

In the kitchen, Breea helped me unpack the mini-pizza crusts, pizza sauce, and mozzarella cheese and we wiped off gritty cans of sliced black olives that had been strewn on the pavement. My daughter's sea green eyes got wider and sparkled with anticipation at our upcoming dinner. First I had to cut the tightly cinched cord from the stray dog's neck and feed the four-legged beggars.

"Go put your backpack in your room," I said, "and I'll meet you back here in the kitchen."

Breea hesitated.

"What's the matter, baby?" I asked, kneeling to brush a few golden hairs off her forehead.

"Mommy," she said, "I'm scared of those people outside the window last night."

She had run from her bedroom into the living room the night before, claiming to have seen several sets of eyes staring in out of the darkness through her bedroom window. I'd gone to her room and looked outside the window with a flashlight, but there was no one there. The diagnosis was an overactive imagination, but I'd let Breea sleep in my bed for the rest of the night. Now, on the following evening, she vividly recalled what she swore she had seen.

I set the dog bowl down just outside the front door and walked into her room with her, putting her schoolbooks on her dresser. The room was in its usual state of disarray, from three little girls (two were my roommate's children who were there a few days a week) sharing a room. Dolls, books, and crayons were strewn around as usual. I pulled back the gossamer curtain and peered out the window into the sunset. Breea wasn't in the habit of making things up. *Weird*, I thought as I let the thin curtain fall gently back into place.

BREEA and I ran into the living room and plopped down on the couch for our sunset ritual. She grabbed the heel of one of my black leather boots, pulling as hard as she could. When it separated from my foot with a loud pop, I forced an exaggerated exhale and Breea landed on the floor on her butt, shrieking with laughter. She did the same thing with the other boot that seemed to have molded to my foot during the day. The pop sent her flying backward again as we laughed together.

I looked out the grand picture window that overlooked the city. I could make out the darkening band of the ocean in the far distance. Breea's and my conversation at the end of a day usually started the same way. "So, how's life?" I'd ask.

"You're so silly, Mommy," she'd answer.

"No roommates tonight," I reminded Breea. "It's just you and me."

"Oh yeah!" Breea grinned, her rolled fist jerking backward toward her hip in a childish gesture of triumph. She was seven and growing up fast. I checked the digital clock on the cable box. The red numbers read 7:20 PM. On the coffee table was Breea's new bright pink Game Boy.

"How about a little Super Mario before dinner?" I suggested. The excited look on Breea's face said it all. "How come you're only seven," I told her as we settled back on the sofa to play with her Game Boy, "and you're better at this than I am?"

She smiled and said nothing, deep in concentration, the tip of her little pink tongue sticking out from the side of her mouth—until a thundering noise erupted from the back of the house.

THE sound of wrenched hinges and tortured wood echoed through the walls. Breea and I spun around in the direction of the thundering crash, just in time to see splintered pieces of wood from the back door frame sail through the air and scatter across the floor. The door flew open, slamming against the solid oak entertainment center just behind it. Three masked gunmen emerged from the darkness, spilling through the door, dressed in black from head to toe. Their heavy black boots pounded violently across the floor toward Breea and me. *This isn't happening. This isn't real,* I told myself.

In an instant, our old life was over, replaced by a new and horrifying reality. Everything was happening in slow-motion frames, one more sickening than the last. I darted my glance to the side to see Breea running toward my bedroom. I tried to get up and go with her when the sharp cold barrels of two handguns pressed into my temples.

"No, no, no!" I screamed, as the thinnest gunman headed for the area where Breea had just disappeared. Grabbing her by her hair near the bathroom adjacent to my bedroom, he dragged her into the living room and shoved her little face to the floor.

A large, muscled hand gripped a handful of my hair so hard I felt it rip away from my scalp. A heavy, thick knee pressed into my back, driving my face cruelly to the dark brown carpet. An unfamiliar metallic taste filled my mouth, the taste of fear. *"Breea!"* I screamed. She was nowhere to be seen and all my reason fled. Visions of rape, torture, and death assaulted me as these three phantoms ominously buzzed round me, like a swarm of angry wasps.

"She's all I have," I heard myself saying. "Please don't hurt her. Please. Please."

"Shut up bitch, or we'll pistol-whip you in front of your kid!" a voice growled. I smelled his sour stench right through his clothing as I tried to lift my head. The iron hand pressed harder into the back of my neck, while a boot's bulky sole positioned itself in front of my nose. I inhaled worn vinyl and rubber.

"Are you going to kill my mommy and me?" I heard my daughter ask in a voice that was weak, shaken, and more childlike than I'd heard in years. I breathed in a sob of relief and a nose full of carpet fibers. *She's alive! Thank God!* I wanted to look at her, see her eyes, touch her face, and calm her fear. I ached to let her know with a single glance that we would be all right. But I didn't know if that was true.

The man holding me down wouldn't let me pick up my head. Beneath the pounding of my heart, I heard someone unrolling and ripping what sounded like tape. From my prone position, I raised my eyes to see four black dog paws, pacing with agitation.

"Voodoo," a raspy voice called out. "Sit!" The Rottweiler wasn't a stray at all. His name was Voodoo and he was theirs, sent here to intimidate us, to soften us for the kill. I'd fed him, petted his head! He circled me now, breathing heavily, drooling and panting.

"I'll do anything," I pleaded with the masked strangers, "but please don't hurt my daughter."

"Shut the fuck up before we beat you so bad you never get up!" someone said. "Besides," he added, "no one can hear you scream way out here, you dumb white bitch. Just do what we tell you and no one will get hurt. Did you know we've been watching you get undressed every day for weeks?" he said.

"For *months*, man," added a low voice. "Damn! What I'd like to do to you. Such a fine white ass you got, lady!"

The large man drove his knee harder into my back while he deftly bound my wrists with duct tape. I strained against the tape but I couldn't move my hands.

"I'd like to give it to you right now," said the man standing near my face. "All those things I saw you do with your boyfriend. You know, the guy with dark hair you had over here a while back. Bitch, you *do* look good walkin' around your house all naked and shit."

I scrunched my eyes tightly closed. When I was as young as Breea, I believed that if I couldn't see my dad abusing my mother, then they couldn't see me.

"Yeah," he went on, "we seen you. You ever had a black man?"

My stomach lurched. Terror overwhelmed me, but I said nothing. I was too busy praying.

"You know you want it," he continued in a sickly

sweet voice that made me, a committed peacemaker, want to turn his own gun back on him and feed him a bullet right down his throat.

"Don't worry, bitch," he said. "We ain't here to rape you. Not tonight. We're not stupid enough to leave DNA at the scene of a dumb white girl's house."

My daughter was in earshot. Did she understand what they were saying to me? I hoped not, as I listened to a pair of footsteps stomping around heavily, heading toward the kitchen, down the hallway, and finally into the southernmost part of the house. I heard the sound of drawers opening in my bedroom. He was looking at my things. I wanted him out of my world, as if his glance would taint my belongings and make them unclean.

Someone turned off all the lights. The entire house hovered in a pall of blackness and fear, where it would remain for the rest of the night. "Do you know why we're here?" asked the talker, the stocky one whose feet were next to my head.

"No," I replied in a cracking voice. Fiber from the carpeting rose into my nose and mouth, choking me.

"You're the bank manager from down the street. We want the money in the vault and you're going to get it for us—or your little girl will die while you watch and you'll be next. Now, I'm going to ask you some questions. We already know the answers so you better not lie. We're testing you and you know what'll happen if you lie. Right?"

I whimpered in response.

"Who's coming to visit here tonight?" was the first question.

"No one." I struggled to be heard with my face buried in the carpet.

"You better not be lying," my tormentor said. "We know everything that goes on in your personal life and at the bank. So you better tell the truth. How many people does it take to get money out of the vault?"

"Two."

"That's right," he said. "How much money gets delivered there every day?"

"I don't know. Someone else orders the amounts."

"About how much?" His voice was loud and angry.

"Two hundred thousand, I guess."

"There better be more than that. We need eight hundred thousand."

"That's impossible," I said, finding my voice. "We're a small branch. We never hold that much money, I swear. We don't even hold half of that. You're holding up the wrong—"

"You better give it all to us," he interrupted me, "'cause if you don't, we'll come back and kill you and your pretty lil' blonde girl. We're going to stay here all night with you to make sure you get that piece of information locked inside your fucking head. Now tell me the name of the little Mexican girl who handles the merchant window in the bank."

"Maria." They already knew.

"What color is her car?"

"Maroon."

"And what does she do when you both get there in the morning?"

"She helps me open the bank and we go into the vault together when we need cash for tellers' windows." Where was my daughter? I hadn't heard her voice in several minutes.

The gunman continued, "You're going to get Maria to go into the vault and help you, just like you always do. By the way, we know where she lives and that she has a new baby. Real cute little thing. So I guess she'll do whatever you ask her, won't she? Your people at the bank respect you and listen to you, don't they? We know 'cause we've been casing the place for a while."

"What have you done with my daughter?" I asked.

"Mommy!" I heard Breea's voice. "I'm over here, Mommy." She sounded close. I assured God I didn't care what happened to me, as long as He kept her safe.

The man held me down with one hand, grabbed a nearby cordless phone with the other and ripped out the battery. I heard someone emptying my purse. My eyes darted across the carpet at floor level to see large gloved hands taking my wallet and removing the battery from my cell phone. They asked about the blue Cherokee that was usually parked in my driveway.

"It belongs to my roommate but she's out until late," I said, praying she would stay over with a friend. Thank God her children were with their father for the week.

"Your boyfriend better not come up here tonight, lady, 'cause he's gonna get a big surprise." He made a

terrible dark scratchy sound, as if laughing were un-
natural to him. Was there any way out of here? My
mind searched for a possible escape, but there was
none. My daughter and I were bound, body and mind,
hostage to desperate strangers.

The talker said, "I know you drink red wine and
you go to the little store down the street for ice cream.
Hell, you almost ran into me at the mall the other day.
You're the hardest bitch I ever tracked 'cause you
drive too fast and I was followin' you so close. I even
know what you ate at the Italian restaurant the other
night. I was in there, too, just watchin' you, lady. And
watchin' you have sex with your man. We saw you in
the living room and in your bedroom. Damn, bitch, I
was wishin' that was me, all up on you like that."

I was working hard to keep from trembling but I
wasn't doing a very good job. My stomach felt hollow
and my head pounded with disgust and rage. Tears and
snot were soaking the brown carpet beneath my face,
running down the cracks of my lips and into my
mouth. My daughter was silent. If I could raise my
head, just enough to see her face . . . I asked them to
please let me sit up.

One of the men grabbed my taped wrists and jerked
me upward, spinning me around on the carpet, burning
the skin on my knees. I didn't care because now I
could see Breea, lying facedown on the floor near
where my feet had just been, with silver duct tape on
her wrists and ankles. A gun was pointed at her head.

"Run, baby, run," I wanted to cry out, but neither of us could do anything.

"Are you okay, baby?" I asked.

"I've stopped shaking, Mommy," she said bravely, tearing my heart in two.

The taller man came out of my bedroom and into the living room, waving around a Victoria's Secret red lace thong. "Let's see you put this on and do your thing right now," he said. Lust oozed from his voice.

Shame and fear colored my face. I shuddered with revulsion that strangers were touching my underwear, invading the most intimate parts of my life. These people had been stalking me for months and I'd never seen any of them. How could that be? Was it my fault? Why hadn't I been more alert? I barraged myself with admonitions that I couldn't have kept my daughter safe from these monsters.

At least I could see them now that I was on my knees, but I couldn't make out much in the dark. Of the three men, one stood out clearly as the leader of the pack. Short and stocky, he held a long, thin-barreled handgun in his right hand.

The second one, a huge linebacker-size man, held the same kind of handgun in his right and was near the dining room emptying the contents of a duffel bag near his feet.

The third, a man of medium height and skinny as a rail, carried a short-barreled handgun. All three were masked, their faces completely hidden, but their eyes flashed from holes cut into knitted beanies and one of them seemed to be wearing a distorted Halloween mask of some kind.

I vowed to notice everything about each of them, their walks, their heights and weights, and the sound of their voices. It was the only sense of control I could grab onto. The torn skin on my knees stung as I studied the taller quiet man where the dark skin on his neck was exposed. A pair of nearly black, hollow eyes glared through the holes in the mask. This was the one who had searched through the house. Beside him was the contents of the black duffel bag—some large arrowlike objects that looked like spears and a blue plastic grocery bag wrapped around something bulky—laid out in a straight line.

The animated, wiry man who stood over my daughter with a gun was excruciatingly thin, his Halloween mask accentuating a pointed chin. I continued to take mental notes of everything: what each man was wearing, the brands of their clothing if I could determine it, the carelessly cut eyeholes in the masks, the rough dark skin on the neck of the apparent leader, and the types of weapons each man carried.

The talker was clearly the mastermind, ordering the others around as he walked over to the dining room table and reached for the blue plastic bag. It rustled as he pulled out two brick-colored long sticks with yellow and red wires attached, the whole thing held together with black tape. "Do you know what this is?" he asked me.

"It looks like dynamite," I said quietly.

"You're not as dumb as I thought," he said. "That's exactly what it is. I have three of these. One for you, one for your little girl, and one for your roommate when she gets home. See this little button?"

He pointed to a gold, circular device with a small button in the center that looked like a doorbell. "This is the detonator," he said, clearly enjoying scaring me. "One wrong move and BANG!" His voice made me jump. "You and your little girl disintegrate." He moved his arms in a sweeping gesture as if he were performing a magic trick.

"*Abra Cadabra*!" the third gunman chimed in. "It'll be just like the Fourth of July around here. Nothin' but fireworks! Day-yam!" The possibility of watching us get annihilated clearly excited him.

"I have to go to the ladies' room," I said. I was telling the truth. I felt sick to my stomach and I was afraid I would soil my pants.

The tall man looked to the leader for the okay. Once he got it, he began to remove the tape from my hands and feet.

"I'll take her, Big Hershey," said the talker. "You stay with the kid."

He untaped my hands from behind my back, re-taped them in front of my body and followed me to the bathroom. He walked so closely behind me, I could hear him breathing. I felt his eyes ogling my rear end as I stepped into the bathroom and automatically reached for the light. He didn't stop me. The glare of the overhead light blinded me for a second since we'd been sitting in the dark for so long, but in a moment my eyes adjusted. I reached up under my long gray business skirt to pull down my panties. There he stood, with his legs wide apart, gripping his gun and watching me. I kept my glance on the floor while he was ripping away my dignity, piece by piece. My bowels were uncontrollable and my stomach was afflicted with revulsion. I was mortified and wanting to finish so I could be with Breea. Why couldn't this pig turn around?

I allowed my eyes to wander—first to the floor, the length of the floorboard, and then to his worn, black Doc Martens. I cautiously began to examine his covered body and face. He had made a mistake when he let me turn on the light. In one split second, my eyes locked with his. I'd seen those eyes before, but where? I looked into the red, bulging, droopy pools. There was no doubt. It was the same man who had come into my bank earlier that day . . .

HE had sat in a rude kind of slouch as I shifted uneasily in my black leather captain's chair, staring at an extremely unpleasant-looking man. It was partly the way he had positioned his thick, stocky body—halfway falling off the chair, his pelvis jutting up and forward, his nervous hands folded in his lap. But it was also the tacky black vest with shiny gold embroidery. I found his lack of an undershirt in bad taste, as the dark fuzz on his chocolate-colored skin stuck out from the center of the vest and under his strongly muscled arms. He handed me a business card that read, "On the Spot Photography by Christopher Butler."

His boorish posture and partially naked chest, although repulsive, could be overlooked, but his eyes could not. Droopy, watery, and bulging, shot with red veins, they made me feel exposed and unsafe. I kept my cool like I'd been trained to do, holding his gaze as he spoke, hoping that someone in the bank would need me so I could get away from this guy. No such luck. I continued to schmooze with him, using the best corporate attitude I could muster.

Relief came about an hour later, when Christopher Butler's girlfriend, a woman to whom he'd been referring, entered the bank. "Hey Lisa," he called out. She came to stand at his side.

Butler remained sitting while Lisa looked around for a chair. *A real gentleman*, I thought as I jumped up and found an empty chair. I pushed it next to the man with the bulging eyes, and Lisa sat.

"Hello," I said. "I'm Michelle." I extended my hand.

She made no motion to shake my hand. I awkwardly returned it to my side and sat back down. Lisa addressed her boyfriend like I wasn't there. "Hey Chris, you missed your three o'clock. I tried to call you on the radio, you know, but you didn't answer."

"Left it in the car," he said.

Lisa looked annoyed. Hiding beneath a masculine demeanor, she was a tall, withered Caucasian woman with a harsh face, an edge to her voice, and a tough exterior that she wore like a shroud. Butler introduced us formally. "Michelle, this is Lisa Ramirez. She's my girl." He looked sullen when he said that.

"Shake hands with her, Lisa," he ordered. "How often do we get to do business with such a nice bank manager?"

Lisa and I shook hands. Her cynical expression was unchanging, as if smiling were such an alien concept, her face had forgotten how to do it. She seemed hollow and I felt growing tension in my body. I forgot all about her, though, when Butler picked up a photo of Breea from my desk. I froze.

"She's a little beauty," he said, tracing her face with his fingers.

"Thank you," I said in my most businesslike voice, quickly taking the photo out of his hands. I held it to my chest, praying that this man and his creepy girlfriend would get the hell away from me. At the beginning of our conversation, Butler had told me he was new in town, he was coming into some money, and he was considering opening an account in this bank. I attempted to bring the conversation back to banking, when Butler and Lisa suddenly stood. "We gotta go but don't worry," he muttered, "we'll see you again *real* soon." And they left the building, with me hoping they'd never return.

I tossed Christopher Butler's business card into the top right-hand drawer of my desk with a bunch of other potential clients. Then I sped out to my car to go get Breea while the bizarre encounter replayed in my mind as I drove through the winding back roads of Vista.

I T had been five hours since the man's eyes and mine had met for the first time.

Look away! Don't let him know you recognize him . . . don't let him know . . . I repeated to myself silently. Any sign that I recognized him and we would surely die. I recognized his voice, too, and now, I could make out his very broad shoulders from under his disguise. His poorly cut ski mask was too small, revealing patches of rough, flaking, dark skin on his neck. He was African American, as was one of his cohorts, and I strained to make out more details without alerting him that I was watching him.

He leaned against the blue and white bathroom tiles. I noted that he was thirteen and a half tiles in height. I looked behind me at the window that led into the parking area and imagined running down the driveway. It would be a clean dash to freedom, but it was impossible with Breea captive in the other room.

"Damn. What's takin' you so long? Come on and finish yo fuckin' business, bitch."

The man's voice jolted me like a bolt of lightning. I reached for the toilet paper roll, wiped myself with embarrassment and disgust, and pulled up my panties. He led me back to the living room and shoved me onto the couch next to Breea, who was staring straight ahead with a frozen expression. I touched her, smelled her hair, and kissed her forehead. I whispered in her ear, "Everything will be okay, baby. Don't worry, Mommy is right here." I wanted to wail but I knew it wouldn't help us out of this mess and it might make the creeps nervous. God only knew what they would do if they were agitated.

I couldn't stop the tears from streaming down my face as the talker moved painfully close to me. "If you try to escape or try anything funny, there are six people outside to make sure you both suffer a slow death," he hissed into my face. His eyes darted to Breea and back to me. I could barely make out his words anymore. They were bleeding together like a long, sharp stab wound, terrible sound after terrible sound.

I heard static as the talker pulled a walkie-talkie out of his dark clothing. It was a female voice on the other end, which I recognized—Lisa Ramirez, the woman who had been in the bank with Butler a few hours ago. "Money One here. What is it Money Two?" he said, lifting the silver two-way Audiovox radio to his lips. Apparently, they had code names. *Not very creative ones,* I thought.

"Money Two calling Money One," the woman's voice said. "Where are you, Chris?" Big mistake. When I heard her call him by name, I knew for certain it was Lisa.

"We're in," Chris told her. "Where are you now?"

The female voice reported she was waiting on Foothill, the closest cross street. "Over and out," she said.

He looked at me and said, "See? All I have to do is

push this button and I can talk to my people outside. They'll do exactly what I tell them, so don't try anything stupid. Now, I'm going to tell you exactly what you gonna do lady, step by step, a hundred times if I have to. You got five minutes to get the money out of the vault after the armored truck makes the deposit in the morning and leaves the parking lot. You gonna put the money like we want it, with no funny business . . ."

I began to mentally disappear, teetering on the brink of panic. My mind searched desperately for a place of peace, an inner silence that would allow me to breathe and think. I instantly recalled a visualization exercise from a book I'd recently read, *Live the Life You Love* by Barbara Sher. The chapter was called "Gather Your Allies" and it discussed the difference between standing alone in times of uncertainty and having someone stand beside you. The exercise was to imagine people you admired or loved standing all around you, powerful forces that you could call into service to bolster you whenever they were needed. I listed them in my mind now, and imagined placing them in locations all around the house.

Jesus stood near the fireplace, reminding me to stand strong in my faith. I placed Breea on the other side of me as she told me that I could do anything. I envisioned my mom and Naomi Judd sitting on the couch, representing strength and dedication to their children. Over by the window stood Oprah Winfrey, deep in compassion and filled with wisdom that only comes from the will to chase your biggest dreams.

Photographer Linda McCartney, an idol of mine, sat near the front door, reminding me to keep my eyes focused on the beauty in the world, even if others didn't see it. And finally, Albert Einstein sat at the kitchen table, telling me there is never a good time to quit. A few more people made my list of allies complete.

"Mommy," Breea called out, her voice jolting me back into the present. "Everything is going to be okay. Don't cry Mommy. I know you're going to do everything right just like they tell you and keep us safe. You can stop crying now Mommy. Just be brave and never give up."

I didn't even know the tears were running down my cheeks. How could she be so strong at a time like this? Her words bolstered me as I waited to see the intruders' next moves. Would they remain relatively calm all night or would it end in some kind of deadly violence?

I was no stranger to violent rages. My father, a hot-headed New York Italian, abandoned in an orphanage by his parents, had given me plenty of experience in placating angry men. Tapping into my childhood survival skills, it was about 10:30 PM when I started making little jokes with the gunmen, to lighten things up, just like I did with my dad.

"Make sure you leave money on the counter for all the food you're eating," I called into the kitchen with a humorous lilt to my voice. I could hear them crunching potato chips and gulping Pepsi from the bottles and orange juice from the carton. *Go ahead,* I thought, *and leave plenty of evidence for the police.* I said nothing further, hoping that maybe if they thought I was "cool," they would abort their plans because Breea and I were good people.

It was almost midnight when I heard a car pull into the driveway. It was Allison, my roommate. I wished to God Breea and I had gone with her to the softball game, but in the end, we'd have ended up in the same position, anyway. It just would have started later.

"Lie facedown on the couch and pretend to be asleep!" the men ordered Breea and me. "Don't move!"

The engine stopped, the car door opened and slammed shut, and Allison's key turned in the lock. I tried frantically to reach her telepathically, to warn her to go away and get help. I heard her intoxicated voice greeting Voodoo, the dog decoy.

"Hi nice widdle doggie. Another stray . . . Hey Michelle! What's with the new dog?" Then she screamed. I opened my eyes to see them dragging Allison toward her bedroom, her mouth covered with a large, gloved hand. The next thing I knew, she was being shoved onto the couch beside Breea and me, screaming for them to get out of her house.

The talker shoved the barrel of his gun up her nose. My arm automatically tried to push the gun away. "Please," I pleaded. "Don't hurt her. She's been drinking. It was the last game of the season. I promise she'll calm down."

"Don't you ever try to touch this gun again, bitch," he snarled at me, "or I'll blow your fucking head off."

The gun swung in my direction and pressed against my face.

"Okay, okay," I muttered as I recoiled. "I'm sorry."

I looked over my shoulder to see Breea curled up in a tight ball, wedged into the corner of the couch, pale as a ghost, silent and wide-eyed. She was in shock as she watched one of the men shove Allison to the floor on her belly and tape her wrists and ankles. Allison pleaded with them to stop. The men paced nervously, darting their eyes from Allison to each other, holding up their spears and pointing them in our faces to scare us even more. It was working.

"Tell her we haven't been like this all night. Tell her!" the talker ordered me. "She's making us real mad."

There was nothing I could say to Allison because she was too drunk to hear me. I just kept watching the men as closely as I could, making a mental picture of every detail. I catalogued their arsenal of spears and I took great care to listen to each man's voice individually so I could distinguish one from the other later—if there was going to be a later. I noted the weapons they'd placed on the dining room table were now pointing in our faces. The spears were black with orange and red colors woven into the neck, leather pieces dangling from their ends. Once the ordeal was over, I would learn that the spears were meant for our dogs if they didn't behave. Thank God they didn't use them.

I have no idea how much time had passed when

they hiked Allison up to sit in a dining room chair near the entrance of the kitchen. The ringleader paced our surreal world in which a wrong move or a bad attitude could mark the end of the lives of my daughter, me, and Allison. Breea and I huddled together on the couch, bound and frightened, while we heard one of the intruders continue to rummage through our stuff in the back of the house.

The other two men sat tall on chairs that looked like perverted thrones, placed in a half-circle. They were savoring their greatest hour—being in control of two helpless white women, a little girl, and a house filled with things they wanted that did not belong to them. *Greedy cowards,* I thought to myself. Well, they may have had control of our bodies and our possessions, but God had control over our destiny. And I was counting on Him to win.

2. A Night in Hell

A saccharine odor turned my stomach as one of our captors lit up a joint. When he turned his back and lifted his mask to take a drag, I tried to catch a glimpse of his face, but he was too careful. He turned up the stereo, loud. It was rap music, and I prayed that Breea would not wake up. She'd finally dozed off in my arms after I'd convinced the leader to remove the tight tape that was making her fragile body so sore. She whimpered when I shifted her in my lap. It was 2:00 AM.

I closed my eyes as the men started tossing sexually explicit language at me again. After rifling through my things, they'd brought a black lace bra into the room, spinning it around one finger. The squirmy one with the foul odor seeping from under his clothes started in again. "We watched through your window," he said, "when you and your man was doin' the wild thing. Man, I'd love a piece of that action. Come on. Let's see some of that."

"Would you please not smoke pot in front of my child," I said, pretending their sexual references were nonexistent. The skinny one took a drag on the joint and blew it out in defiance as he described what he wanted to see Allison and me do to him and which parts of our bodies he wanted us to use.

I held my daughter tighter, thinking about how much the carpet needed cleaning and the plants needed watering. I recalled Breea's upcoming doctor's appointment, anything to drown out the threats and the pounding music.

"Hey, Joker," the leader addressed his lanky cohort. He gestured toward me. "Wouldn't you like some of that? By the way, you girls can call us the Joker, the Riddler, and the Penguin."

Allison, still sitting beside me, suddenly joined in the bantering, trying to lighten up the atmosphere. She joked with them, trying to convince one of the guys to take off his mask. He refused. I stood up, lay Breea on the couch, and started pacing. They allowed me to do that, and in the next few minutes, they began talking to me like I was a human being, albeit their prisoner.

"I have a girlfriend," the ringleader said almost thoughtfully. "She's white." He sat on the edge of the coffee table in front of me.

The skinny one chimed in, "You're one of the coolest bitches I ever met. Too bad we have to do this to you. You may not understand, but we ain't got no choice. See, it's like this. I got a newborn with a bitch that trapped me in Chicago." He laughed rudely.

So far, I knew that the skinny one lived in Chicago at one time, and the ringleader had a white girlfriend— Lisa. And the big guy had a nickname, Big Hershey. Studying them gave me somewhere to place my concentration while they ransacked my home and dreamed without conscience of their stolen loot. The big one would leave the room, go rummaging through our things, and then he'd stride into the room, throwing the latest item onto a pile they intended to steal. So far, they had gathered my Canon video camcorder; my Sony Walkman and CD player; a load of my favorite CDs; credit cards; camera equipment; and a few pieces of jewelry, not expensive but sentimental. My things.

The leader rifled through my videos and put one into my VCR, *The Perfect Storm*. He turned down the music, thank God, while I stood at the window, gazing out as the television set flickered. Boats rocked on a turbulent sea. I watched the city lights wash the hillside homes in a cozy glow, where people were resting peacefully in their beds. I would trade places with any one of them. If only one person somewhere knew what was happening to us and could rescue us from our living hell . . .

"Mommy," Breea's squeaky voice called out from the couch. "I wanna lie in your bed."

I walked over to her as calmly as I could and picked

her up. "I'm taking her into my room," I said. "Please don't stop me."

Daybreak was four hours away and I hadn't slept a wink. Now I needed to hold Breea in the comfort of my bed, the place where we had our cherished snuggle time. The ringleader didn't stop me but he followed us into the bedroom, his glare burning a hole straight through me. Breea and I lay on the bed as I stroked her hair, savoring her sweet breath while we held on to each other in the eerie silence. With a masked, armed man staring at my daughter and me from a chair at the end of my bed, I drifted into a semi-unconscious state for what seemed to be mere seconds.

A filmy coating covered my tongue as my eyes struggled to open on a brisk fall morning. I felt a gnawing anxiety in my gut. My mind searched for an explanation. It had been one of my brother's birthdays the day before and I hadn't gotten him a gift. He was a hard person to buy for, he just didn't care about "things" very much, so I'd probably get him one of those "I love and appreciate you" Hallmark cards and slip a twenty-dollar bill inside. None of my four brothers were very attached to birthdays so it didn't really . . .

"Time to get up." A rough voice grated in my ear.

A metallic taste that felt like rising vomit burned my gut as I catapulted straight up in my bed in a cold sweat. My heart sank when I realized this was not a dream. My eyes welled up and I tightened my hold on Breea who was rustling beside me. The sheer white fabric that covered my windows undulated in the morning breezes that blew up from the canyon below. I thought those curtains were romantic when I bought them. Each morning, I'd gently awaken and see the ocean right through them, a patch of crystal clear blueness that lay beyond the heavy stone retaining wall in the front of the home I loved so much.

If this were a dream about taking a mistaken turn at a fork in the road, I could go back and fix it. But last night was no horror movie. It was real, in my face and unavoidable, like the sun that was about to rise in the eastern sky, as if it were a regular day.

"Breea, honey. Wake up baby," I whispered. I inhaled her hair and caressed her soft skin. Her eyes opened, appearing more beautifully turquoise green than the ocean outside the window. If this were my time to die, so be it, but it was not her time. No child should be put through the kind of pain she was experiencing. She was only seven years old, for God's sake! Rage flew up my spine. My emotions hardened into a cold ball of ice, a stoic determination rising from my fury. I would get through this with no mistakes. This was the mind-set I needed, one of absolute commitment to do everything they told me to do—perfectly. Then I would help put the pathetic creeps behind bars for the rest of their lives.

"Go take a fuckin' shower," the stocky man ordered me, grabbing my sore and bruised wrists. He was clearly agitated. "Do all the things you normally do to get ready for work. Fix your hair and wear them business clothes you got."

Breea looked more terrified than ever as I swept her up in my arms. "I'm too scared to cry, Mommy," she said. Tears streaked my face as I headed for the shower.

"Where do you think you're taking her?" the man asked. The talker's voice was shaky, on the edge of panic, a lot less confident than it had sounded last night.

"She and I always shower together in the morning," I said. It was a lie and I hoped they hadn't been watching me closely enough or early enough in the mornings to know it. I just couldn't let go of her, not yet. Not now.

He let me take her into the bathroom. I started to close the door and he shoved my arm away, watching our every move as I turned on the shower. I slid my clothes to the floor and concealed Breea's naked body with my own, trying to use the Plexiglas door as a shield. The warm water poured over us and I raised my eyes to the ceiling, trying to get my wits about me. I was not tired, even though I'd only dozed off for about twenty minutes during the night. My adrenaline was pumping and terror coursed through me as I let the water mask the tears that were running down my face. I could make out the gunman's shadowy figure through the steamed glass panel of the metal-trimmed shower door.

Breea clung to my naked hips, the wet droplets pausing at her long eyelashes and falling to the tile floor. The man tapped on the shower door with his gun and we both jumped.

"We ain't got all day," he said. "Let's go."

I stroked Breea's hair back from her drenched face and turned off the water. We stepped out of the shower naked and exposed. The door hinge complained with a squeaking sound and Breea stayed behind the shower door as I reached for a towel. The gunman stared right at us, his feet about a shoulder width apart as he gripped his black handgun. Breea stood behind me, peering out from behind my right side. How dare he put my daughter through this. I rushed to cover her bare body with a bath towel and then I covered my own. I wanted to crumble to the floor in a ball and scream for mercy, but that would do nothing for either Breea or me. Acknowledging the extent of the danger we were in, I resented these men for how badly my little girl would feel about life and about men after this.

And what about me? I would never feel the same about men, my body, or my privacy. I closed my eyes tightly, massaging my sore wrists and then putting the towel up to my face with both hands. I tried to focus on what I had to do next, moving with a crawling numbness, feeling less than human as I found familiar clothes for us to wear. The talker left while I blow-dried my hair, but he returned in a moment holding the dynamite sticks, the duct tape, and the remote control detonator he had shown me last night. The tall, quiet one followed closely behind him. He unplugged my blow-dryer.

"Turn around and pull up your shirt," the ringleader harshly ordered.

Breea was fully clothed now, sitting close to me on the bathroom counter. I pulled up my shirt, grasping onto the cold tile countertop with my hands while the men used duct tape to strap the red sticks to my back. Bursts of anger exploded in my brain as fear crawled under my skin like maggots. The dynamite sticks stuck sharply into my spine as the foul smell of body odor and the sound of ripping duct tape nauseated me. He was taping me so tightly, my rib cage felt constricted. "Please loosen it," I pleaded. "I can't breathe."

He ignored my pleas and approached my daughter with two more sticks of dynamite. I struggled with the kind of rage that makes a woman go crazy and pull out her hair. I wanted to stab him with something— anything to keep him from touching my baby. When they lifted up my daughter's shirt to tape explosives on her tiny back, I can say without hesitation that if someone had put a gun in my hand at that moment, I would have shot that man dead.

Breea was shaking as her hands gripped the sides of the toilet seat for balance while they finished taping the dynamite. She whimpered softly, "Mommy, it hurts so bad. It's digging into my side and I can't breathe. Please make them take it off, please."

I turned to the faceless man and began to scream, "Loosen the fucking tape on her. Please!"

He gestured to the tall man to retape Breea. "Now shut up and wear this," he said, throwing a loose-fitting tan sports jacket at me. He'd chosen it from my closet while I was in the shower. Trancelike, I put it on. "Now turn around," he said. I turned my back toward him. "Yeah, that works," he mused, referring to the fact that the jacket hid the explosives from view. "Now go sit in the living room. I'll tell you when it's time."

I took Breea's hand and we walked slowly into the living room, bearing our delicate burdens on our backs.

"If you try to take off the tape or the dynamite," the talker reminded me, "the thing will detonate. We wouldn't want the little girl to be an orphan, would we?"

"What did they put on me, Mommy?" Breea asked.

"Just something to keep track of you sweetie." I didn't want her to know. I wanted to make it better for her somehow, to make it unreal. But it *was* real and all I could do was pray we didn't end up in a million pieces as I sat helplessly on the living room couch. Allison was on a chair across the room where they had ordered her to sit. She suddenly called out to me in a loud whisper, "Call the police the minute you get to work."

I cringed, wondering if she'd have been more careful if one of *her* children were in danger. Her behavior the night before was less than rational. I looked at them walking toward Allison. They had overheard her talking about calling the cops. They grabbed Allison and began dragging her toward the back bedroom. They knew I would do nothing outside of their instructions until my daughter was free and I could hold her in my arms, alive.

Daylight was approaching when I saw the skinny guy crawling on his belly like a serpent, moving from one room to the next, afraid of being seen through the window. "We have a bad feeling about Allison so we took care of her," he told me.

Took care of her? What did that mean?

He continued, "She could get us all killed and we don't like her one bit. She's talkin' all nasty and shit, tryin' to get us to take off our masks, tellin' you to call the cops. That bitch is crazy."

I stayed quiet. What could I say?

The talker entered the room. "You have ten minutes to say whatever you need to say to your girl," he told me. "Remember, if you mess up, you'll never see her again. I promise."

Ten minutes to say everything? Impossible. How do you put every word, every emotion, and every dream that had ever come true because of her into ten minutes? How do you explain all the things you wish you could take back or undo or do again? How do you say it all? Ten minutes.

I leaned in as close to her ears as I could get, trying to keep our words private. "You are so special, baby,"

I whispered. "You're everything I ever dreamed of when I chose to be a mommy. God made you perfect for me, did you know that? I love you more than I can say and I'm so proud of you. You are my hero, my angel, and guess what? I'll be back to get you as soon as I can. Okay? It's all going to be fine."

My mind began playing worst-case scenarios. What if I fainted or vomited and couldn't carry out the plan? Would they kill us? What if there wasn't enough money in the vault that day or they panicked and got trigger-happy? What if they actually detonated the dynamite right now and we exploded all over the house?

"I know you're gonna do all the stuff they told you to, Mommy." Breea's voice alerted me that I was losing my concentration. I focused on my daughter's beautiful eyes. "You're tough and brave, remember?" she said to me.

"So are you, sweetie," I answered. "We're going to get through this together, right?"

"Right," she said weakly.

"Remember our song," I said. *Together forever just you and me.*

She joined in. *Together forever that's the way it's meant to be.*

"That's us, Mommy."

"Yup, that's us, and no matter what, it's true. We're together forever. I love you a million times plus eternity."

"Never give up Mommy. Just be brave and everything will be okay." Those were the words I'd told *her* time and again, and now she was repeating them to me. I hugged her, rocking back and forth, kissing her long and hard on the forehead, my hands and arms wrapped tightly around her body and face as I felt the dynamite strapped to her narrow back.

"That's enough," said the talker, his ugly mask lighting up in the glow of the rising sun. "Take her into her bedroom. NOW!"

We walked into Breea's bedroom to find Allison tied up on the bed, tape covering her mouth, eyes, wrists, and ankles. They had successfully silenced her. A pang of guilt overcame me. If I hadn't been a bank manager and hadn't moved in with Allison, none of this would be happening. My job had put my daughter, my roommate, and myself in mortal danger.

"Put her in the closet!" an angry voice ordered. I clutched Breea to my leg as gently as I could. Any movement felt dangerous with the dynamite on our bodies. I gazed into the dark closet. I couldn't allow her to sit in there like that. "Can I give her something to keep her occupied in there, just a little something, you know anything, a crayon and paper—please?"

"Make it quick."

I was frantic, a devoted mommy to the end, if this was the end. I searched nervously for a pad of paper, a pencil, or crayons—anything she could use to write or draw to keep herself busy. Her Game Boy, the one we were playing with just hours before, was still in the living room. "Here baby," I said, handing her a pad of paper that was next to her bed. "Draw a pretty picture or write Mommy a note. I'll be back as soon as I can, sweetie."

"Pinky promise Mommy?" she asked.

"Pinky promise baby." We locked pinkies and I managed a weak smile, hoping she couldn't hear my heart pounding. "Pinky promise angel," I repeated faintly, trying to convince myself. I stood slowly and we used our secret sign language to say, "I love you for eternity."

For the first time, Breea began to really cry. "Mommy, no. Don't leave, Mommy, please . . ."

The talker shoved me toward the door and my daughter's cries faded as I became lifeless, mechanical. I walked out of the bedroom, leaving behind my daughter strapped with explosives, imprisoned in the closet to my right. To my left, my roommate lay on her daughter's bed, strapped with dynamite, bound and gagged. They were both counting on me to keep them alive. I felt the weight of their lives heaped upon me with every step.

Walking felt arduous, as if I were moving in slow motion through something thick and foreboding. I silently repeated the steps they expected me to take, rehearsing their instructions.

"No funny business," a faraway voice reminded me. "No police calls. No alarms. No bait. Just wait for the Brink's truck to do the delivery, put the money in the bag like I told you, and leave the bank within five minutes—or else."

I nodded and got ready to save my daughter's life. On the inside, I was screaming and swooning. On the outside, I was a robot; programmed and switched on, ready to rob my own bank.

3. The Beast Inside

His gloved hand gripped my arm with urgency as my daughter's screams faded.

"I have to do this to you. I wish I didn't have to, but I do. You don't understand." The ringleader was talking in an almost fragile boyish voice as he handed me my briefcase and showed me the black nylon gym bag he'd rolled up and put inside the bag for the money I was meant to steal. He explained how he wanted it stacked—hundreds first, then fifties, and the twenties on top.

He shoved me out the front door, sticking his gun into my back. I headed toward my Jeep as the door slammed behind me. My head pounded as I struggled to make peace with my past. I was preparing to die. He would never know my past nor about the things that I'd survived . . .

• • •

I was six the first time my father drove away in an old beat-up Ford with my surrogate uncle in the backseat. Leaving behind seven children and his broken, battered wife, my father was headed for Southern California.

The next morning was so quiet. I remembered he was gone before I got out of bed. No yelling echoed through the halls and when I wandered into the kitchen, there was no lingering smoke to escalate my asthma. There were only stale cigarette butts in full ashtrays and day-old sheets of the sports page strewn across the table. My dad, the man who called women whores and houseflies little niggers was gone.

The youngest of three girls, I was the middle child of seven. I grew up in a slew of houses that never seemed like homes, on nameless streets in nameless towns. That was how it felt anyway, the possible pleasure of each new location ruined by my father's rigid control and raging outbursts.

Born on the outskirts of Boston, I was ill with asthma as an infant and spent many months at various intervals in a plastic-tented hospital bed, showered with warm, sticky mists to open my throat. Gasping for breath, I got poked and prodded regularly by nurses in crisp white uniforms and white caps. I was isolated most of the time and after a childhood of long, uninterrupted silences, I developed a love of and need for solitude that lasted into my later life.

My father grew up in orphanages. A New York Italian street punk measuring in at five feet two inches on his tiptoes, walked like he was six feet tall, holding high his handsome Italian face. A hardworking man with a bruised ego, he believed in introducing his young children to the harsh reality of the world by beating it into us. My dad, crowned with slicked-back ebony hair, acted on the outside as though he were invincible. But on the inside, he was a broken man.

When I learned to walk, it was over eggshells, aware from an early age that keeping my father calm by following his instructions, no matter how ridiculous they seemed, was of the utmost importance, the key to my survival. As I grew, I learned to predict my father's moods, struggling to accommodate the sting of his hand and the jab to my self-worth amid my mother's agonized weeping.

I never talked back to my father or disagreed with him. That was a sure ticket to abuse, and my mother never stuck up for me. I knew in my heart that she wanted to tell him to stop. I could see it in her eyes. But little did I know or understand that her silence was her attempt to avoid a confrontation. In this stifling and violent atmosphere, my self-esteem slowly deteriorated, leaving nothing but a critical voice hammering home the message to me that I was basically no good. Why else would my dad hit me and call me names every time he got the chance? And why would my mother fail to stop him?

Maybe it was his good looks that initially attracted my mother to him. But more likely than not, it was her disappointing circumstance that drew her to him. She was raised in a fairly wealthy family in a small New England town. A fiery woman with great wit and charm, she had a love for adventure that outweighed good decision making around men. After a six-year affair with a married man twice her age that had started while she was still in high school, she left her small town and had a baby, their baby—a mortal sin back then. Her love child was three months old when she met my dad. It would be thirty years before we all learned the truth.

I tried to stay close to my mom when I was growing up, but she lacked the warmth and earthiness to make a child feel secure. Maybe she was just too damaged herself to be able to provide me with the kind of touching and confidence every child needs and deserves. I know she tried. There were times she took us hiking or let me stay home from school so she and I could listen to Barry Manilow, Neil Diamond, Elvis, or Tom Jones while we danced around the living room—moments I wished would last forever.

But the good times were slim and the disconnection to all other family members from both sides of the parental tree escalated. We never met an aunt, an uncle, or a cousin, and laid eyes on his parents once or twice when I was too young to even remember them. I fantasized that when I got married, I would give my children oodles of love and protection, a permanent home, and the joy of family. I thought I was in charge of my own destiny and circumstances—naiveté at its best.

Just like any other kid, I wanted to know I was loved, and as the verbal and physical abuse continued, I tried harder and harder to make my parents proud of me. I wanted to be Daddy's princess, but instead I was witness to his violent rages and left to feel like the fourth of seven of my parents' mistakes. Holidays in particular were a badly played game in my opinion. Sure we smiled. Sure we acted happy and we ate big meals and opened presents under the tree. But we all knew that our mail-order gifts had been purchased by bad checks that my mother wrote. We also knew that soon enough, the electricity and gas would be turned off and my father would erupt. We tried to keep them out of our minds, but without fail, as soon as New Year's was over, the shut-off notices would arrive and we'd be shivering, hungry, and wandering around in the dark.

On the inside, I guess my dad was a sad little boy struggling with the aftereffects of his own violence, rejection, and abandonment. But his pattern of beating his way through his life and his family, teaching us what he considered "the ropes" of the real world and his perverse definition of respect, made his absence a welcome reprieve.

The pattern was always the same, with a slight variation. We would start to feel somewhat hopeful when we were on our own—until a month or two later when Mom, overwhelmed by raising seven children alone, would give in to the pressures of life without him. When the phone rang, she'd go running back to him, promising us that it would be different this time—only to start the process all over again.

It had been months since he left Boston, headed for the golden state of California. Within a week, Mom packed all seven of us into her tiny red hatchback car with a few of our most precious belongings. She put on a pair of cute white knickers, white dock sneakers, a tank top, and wrapped a bandana around her head and we were off. I remember gazing out of the hatchback window with tears streaming down my face, mourning my childish treasures that now filled the green, overstuffed trash cans as a result of our sudden move. I tried to lose my sadness and fear in my mother's joy as she sang us radio tunes in the car and trilled her beautiful laughter that we heard so rarely. We were heading West, she told us, to be with my dad (and his demons)—in his supposed new-found paradise.

It was on that extended cross-country journey that I learned to love the open road. I savored the sense of freedom and I learned to swallow my tears right over the lump in my throat. A hard-earned lesson, we would all need that kind of control to deal with what was to come when we reached our destination. But during the trip, even though we got lost constantly, my mom made jokes and sang songs to lighten the mood. The freeway ramps in the shape of the number eight were a roller coaster of sorts to me, as I had never seen so many bridges, off ramps, and speeding automobiles. And Mom did not seem to be in that much of a

hurry to get to paradise, which was at best, a large un-
known. The trip was filled with obstacles; breaking
down and getting lost. By the time we hit the big state
of Texas, we were rolling steady and California was
twenty-four hours away.

Meeting up with my dad again was bittersweet for
me. His rental in sunny San Diego wasn't so
bad, although it was too citified for me. I was not
pleased a few weeks later when my parents bought a
little house just ten blocks from the first, in the midst
of an all-black downtown neighborhood on 49th
Street. And let me tell you, the people there did not
take kindly to a gaggle of "white trash" kids and their
parents.

I marveled that as much as Dad professed to despise "niggers," he'd chosen a small stucco house for
the ten of us where we were literally surrounded by
people of color. The white walls were stained yellow
and much of the cheap wall paneling had been removed and never replaced. In the rear of the house, a
staircase with peeling paint led outside to a nasty back
alley where a number of large, foul-smelling trash cans
were picked through every morning by the homeless.

"My life won't be like this forever," I remember
telling myself one night when we were awakened by
rocks being hurled through our windows. I got spit on
in school, I had my hair pulled daily, and I was jeered
by angry African American kids whenever I walked
down the street. We finally packed up and left the

neighborhood amid cheers from our neighbors that we were leaving. We heard the epithets, "White trash, get out of here!" as we drove away. They had won. I will never forget the feeling of being rejected by an entire neighborhood.

We ended up in a small suburb of San Diego, a safer place to live at first. I managed to do well in my studies and deal secretly with Dad's "episodes."

By the time I was thirteen, I secretly started my period without ever having "the talk" with my mom. I used toilet paper to stop the bleeding until I figured out how to use pads and tampons and I gave up on finding the right card for Father's Day. Too many "perfect dad" Hallmark cards announced a ritual I could have done without. I remember running out of the store one day, joking to a friend with tears in my eyes, "They should have a new kind of card for people like me that say, 'Thanks, Dad, for knocking peoples' teeth out in front of me on the side of the road." He was the king of road rage before it even had a name.

While Dad intermittently beat his family into submission and worked long hours at the hospital, he eventually took off to Reno with our permanent house guest, my surrogate uncle. He took money we couldn't spare and would send us photos in a manila envelope. I retrieved one from the mailbox and opened it to see a group of half-naked women holding drinks, surrounding Dad who was wearing a disturbing grin. In the meantime, we had no running water or electricity. We spent countless nights alone while Mom walked to work on her blistered feet. We huddled around the hi-bachi in the backyard, eating out of a blackened pan and using the neighbor's bathroom—until we were evicted. The sheriff who appeared at our door told us to take what we could carry as we kids were separated, scattered in the homes of friends who were willing to take us since we had no money and no place to go.

I went to live with my best friend where the horse in the backyard and a connected family made me feel like I belonged somewhere. Their vegetarian, hippie lifestyle laced with constant pot smoking and nudity agreed with me and music became my great escape. Loaded on pot and listening to Earth, Wind & Fire or Boz Scaggs was the beginning of a world that made sense to me. It was there, in that loving, nonaggressive environment, that I was introduced to the concepts of goodness and faith. The weight of the world melted away when I got high and danced around the living room naked, meditating on positive thoughts. I was starting to develop inner strength, finally surrounded by nonviolent people I could trust.

Sadly, my good fortune was over by the end of eighth grade when I was forced to leave the friends on whom I had counted. Mom took Dad back again and they moved us to a new school forty minutes away from everyone I knew. On the first day of high school—a new girl with hand-me-down clothes and a secret life of abuse at home—it was easy to say yes when a girl offered me a pill. Before I knew it, I was downing Black Beauties (better known as speed) with some of the "cool" kids, just to get through a day.

On a cold, damp afternoon in January 1981, I lost my virginity to an older boy with long, straight blond hair and piercing blue eyes. He wore a rock band T-shirt, torn jeans, and Colorado boots with red laces. A thick silver chain hung from his pocket, attached to a black leather Harley-Davidson wallet, and he followed me to class, walked me home, carried my books, and even told me I was pretty. I was stunned since I was accustomed to being criticized and beaten down by men giving orders. This guy was nice because he liked me—a brand-new concept.

When he climbed on top of me after six months of courting I watched him squirm, moan, and groan with pleasure and I became excited. "Let the games begin!" I thought as I touched his penis and experimented kissing him passionately, his eyes staring right into mine. His out-of-control responses to my actions drove my desire to learn as much as I could about loving and manipulating men. It was the dawning of understanding the extraordinary power a woman could have over a man, if she got the knowledge she needed.

Just before I turned sixteen, I climbed out of my bedroom window one night, ran softly across the wood-beamed patio cover, and jumped down to the earth to freedom. I ran straight into the arms of my first boyfriend, but my illusions were quickly dispelled by his sudden bursts of jealousy and anger. I knew nothing about psychology at the time, but his violent rages reminded me of my father so much, I became disenchanted.

Just like Dad had done with Mom, my first big love began to monitor my every move, my conversations, and even my clothes. When the sweet man who had taken my virginity started to hit me and then apologized, I took him back, just like I'd learned from my mother. His apologies melted me and I craved his love and attention, waiting and hoping for him to return to the boy with whom I'd fallen in love—just like my mother. My escape was school and I enrolled in an after-school Registered Occupational Program (ROP) to become a Certified Nurse's Aide (CNA). While I sold my boyfriend's baggies of pot at his aggressive urging, I tacked on a little extra for myself and stashed it for when I would make my getaway.

One morning when I walked over to kiss him goodbye for the day, he became infuriated, blaming his rage on my teased-up hairstyle and dark makeup. He locked me in the bedroom with him, put a knife to my throat, and when he finally let me go, that was the end of the relationship. I moved out, dropped out of school, and lived homeless on the street for a time, stealing some guy's keys to his truck where I crashed for a few weeks until my guilty conscience made me return it to its rightful owner. Sometimes I crawled into unlocked cars to get out of the cold, dreaming of graduating high school. I finally got a job at Burger King to pay rent on a single room I landed in the ultimate party house. At age seventeen, life was not about a cap and gown for me. It was about survival.

As soon as I received my CNA certificate, I stopped flipping burgers and scrubbing toilets as a night janitor. For my second job as a nurse, I cleaned bedpans and soothed bedsores. But I became emotionally involved with each patient, the majority of whom were elderly, paraplegic, or quadriplegic. I cared too much, I had no ability to detach, and I often brought my work home, particularly with one patient.

Middle-aged and paraplegic, this man walked on his hands because he had no legs and had a small yacht where a host of pretty women visited him every day. When he introduced me to Janice, a gorgeous red-haired stripper friend of his (an exotic dancer as she called it), her stories of glitz, seduction, and financial independence got my attention. I wanted that for myself, but could I do what Janice did? I decided to find out.

She brought me with her to a private bachelor party late one night to begin my training. I watched and learned. What was so bad about showing off your beautiful body to a group of men who appreciated you and paid you money to strut around and act enticing? By the end of the night, when the men cheered and cajoled me to get up and show them what I had, I strutted to the music as twenty-five men chanted my name and threw money at me. Not only did I make my entire month's rent money in one night, I also took center stage and got the male attention that temporarily filled the void in my relationship with my dad.

The feeling of power was heady stuff and I learned to dance in a sexy way that drove men crazy and left them begging for more. This was a new high with a new job that paid four hundred dollars for two hours of flirting. That was a lot more than I'd ever earned and soon it was good-bye to nursing and hello to the world of topless dancing. I would sunbathe by day, dance topless by night, and in between, I did all the drugs I could get my hands on. The best part was being on stage. When the music began to play, I'd close my eyes and escape to anywhere as the rush took over and I could be someone other than Michelle.

For the first time in my life, I didn't feel like a tomboy as I used my feminine wiles to my full advantage. I learned how to tease as I practiced facial expressions in the mirror, trying to look sexy, fun, and alluring. I started going to concerts with my friends, wearing makeup, and fixing my hair in a semiwild, vixen fashion. Men responded, and I collected phone numbers left and right.

Soon enough, I was spending time backstage with friends, hanging out with famous rock stars, riding on their tour buses for weeks at a time, and Hoovering all the free cocaine I could find. The Hollywood party scene at the Roxy, the Rainbow, and the Hollywood Palladium were my stomping grounds. I was an eighties "IT" girl, the very thing my father had accused me of being, long before I knew what the word "slut" meant.

I hid my lack of confidence behind heavy makeup and short skirts. The highs were fabulous, but I ended up feeling weary and disappointed in a life that I had initially labeled "glamorous." What was glamorous about topless dancing to get back at my father, or to get through nursing school to support a family I didn't have? I ran with a crowd in which we understood each other and we didn't judge. But unlike some of the other girls, I had my limits.

For example, one night Janice drove me to a multimillion-dollar mansion on the cliffs above the sea, where she was living with her boyfriend. They offered me a large room with an ocean view, all the house privileges I wanted, an invitation to a very swanky, exclusive "OUI" party in Beverly Hills and no rent.

The catch?

I would give them fifty percent of the money I earned being a high-class call girl. I have to admit that I considered it. They made it sound so wonderful, with government officials and other high-powered clients and outrageous money, but being a hooker, even under the guise of another title, was taking it too far. I told them I'd think about it and an hour or so later, we took a drive to discuss the possibilities. The sun was just setting as we pulled into a gas station and a small voice in my head was nagging me, telling me to run as fast as I could. I jumped out of the car and ran while they were in the minimart, buying Diet Cokes.

I walked to the corner and stood there, confused, fidgeting. They drove the car beside me and rolled down the window. "Come on, Michelle," they urged. "We love you, you know that. Get back in the car."

I'd heard that one before. My dad's voice echoed, "You know I love ya, I love all my kids and their motha. I just have to teach you the ropes"—like we were his opponents in the boxing ring of life.

Now, even after twenty-four hours of sex, LSD, cocaine, pot, and plenty of booze, I knew I had to get away from them. When they saw that I'd made up my mind, they idled a moment and then drove away. There I stood in my miniskirt and a very tight T-shirt, wondering what to do, so I began to walk. To where, I had no idea. I just started to walk. I feared that some lecherous guy might stop for a woman who looked like I did. But instead a van pulled up and stopped. A conservative-looking woman rolled down the window and looked at me with a kindly face. A man was driving, most likely her husband, and they seemed genuinely concerned. At twenty years old, loaded and dressed like a hooker, I was undoubtedly a tragedy in progress.

"Are you all right?" the woman asked.

"No," I blurted, bursting into tears. "I'm not all right."

The next thing I knew, I was in the backseat of this Christian couple's van, feeling perfectly safe even though we had never before laid eyes on each other. They kept me at their home for the next three days, feeding me and reading me Scriptures. I took in the words of God like a starving woman eating her first meal in years. On the fourth day, they helped me find a room to rent in Pacific Beach. From then on, I was drug-free, although I did continue to dance for a living, to pay for training for my next chosen profession—dental school.

Somehow, life was making sense to me for the first time in a very long time. Dancing could provide me with the money I needed for a different kind of work, as soon as I could manage it. In the meantime, I was discovering things I never knew about myself, now that I was sober of mind and spirit. I was finally growing up.

When I turned twenty-one, I met a navy man who made me laugh. And then, it didn't hurt that he was drop-dead gorgeous and I was in love, truly in love for the first time in my life. His name was Jeff, he was my future husband and he was everything I'd ever dreamed about and more. His parents were the parents I'd always wanted and it seemed my life was actually working out. My days as an exotic dancer ended as I put myself through dental assistant training and X-ray technician courses. After knowing Jeff for five months, I married the charismatic navy man turned respiratory therapist and I had the best four years of my life with him.

I quickly found a job as a dental assistant, but pretty soon, the sound of teeth grinding, drills squealing, and saliva suctioning amid sudden angry outbursts from the dentist himself sent me looking for a change. I decided I wanted a corporate environment with a sense of structure, so I started my banking career as a drive-up window teller while I attended banking school. For the next several years, I climbed my way up the male-dominated corporate ladder while Jeff and I lived the American dream, shopping for our first home, hanging out in the desert, riding off-road vehicles with our friends.

But just when I thought I was on the right track, life shattered yet another of my dreams. Jeff's father was diagnosed with cancer and when he died six months later, a part of Jeff went with him, leaving behind a broken, guilt-ridden destructive man. He became addicted to pain pills in the weeks after his dad passed away, his temper flared out of control, and he withheld affection, spending most days languishing on the couch in a stupor. And I was pregnant.

The birth of Breea did nothing to change Jeff. Within six weeks of her delivery, he took a drive to the local Home Depot and didn't come back. When he showed up at our door weeks later, looking like he'd been living in a dumpsite, I encouraged him to check into rehab. To my amazement, he did. Two weeks later, however, he left the facility without a word and disappeared. I sometimes got home in the evenings to find odd car parts on my patio and broken screens. Then one day after work, I found Jeff crouched in the corner of the kitchen.

He had turned to street drugs and his violent, irrational behavior became too much to bear. I called 911. In the weeks to follow, I filed for divorce and took Breea away to make our life somewhere, safe and far away from the person Jeff had become.

I found a temporary home in the mountains near Julian, California, where I saw an announcement in the local paper that a bank was about to open. I applied cold and I got the job! Two months later, they offered me a promotion to work at their corporate offices in the desert town of El Centro as the regional relationship banking manager or, as it's more commonly known, regional sales manager.

With a long list of babysitters and friends who could help me out due to my twelve-hour workday, my daughter grew and thrived. At age thirty, I was promoted to assistant vice president. Marveling at my own progress, with my two-year-old angel by my side, I was finally making enough money in a legitimate way for Breea and me to get by. I was turning our lives around, but the regional position required too much travel. I longed to be with Breea more even if it meant less pay. I began to explore my options.

One day, I was offered an opportunity to participate in the first bank management training program in the western region for one of the largest banks in the country. Buoyed by the encouragement of my friends and a new boyfriend, I accepted. And so, I found myself driving a U-Haul away from the dust and bugs of El Centro until I was breathing the salty air back in San Diego.

When I became bank manager of a small branch that was right down the hill from where we lived, our life thrived. Secure in myself and in my goals, I was on a mission, focused on giving my daughter a quality of life I never had, and making her proud of me. By the time we moved into the house on the hill with our roommate Allison, my divorce was final, my job was secure, I had fallen madly in love with a man in Ohio, and I could breathe easy—until Christopher Butler walked into my bank and turned my new life into a scalding inferno.

4. Robbing the Bank

"GET in!" the leader ordered.

I climbed into the driver's seat of my Jeep. He slammed the door shut and got in the back, pressing the gun into my rib cage, while he stooped low in the backseat. He held the gun on me with one hand, his Audiovox radio was in the other, and the key to our lives—the detonator—was in his pocket. "Money Two," he spoke into the radio. "This is Money One. We are en route. Take your places."

I drove slowly, a rare occurrence for me, fantasizing at every stoplight about rushing into the street and screaming for help. The man in the backseat knew that I wouldn't—not with Breea strapped with dynamite and locked in the closet. I talked myself through what I had to do. There was no way to alert someone without tipping off my captors, since they'd shown me a

microphone and a police scanner attached to the dynamite pack that was weighing so heavily on my back.
They would be aware of my every move and every
word so there was no conceivable way to alert the
police.

I continued to drive slowly, following directives,
suddenly feeling light-headed. I realized that I hadn't
eaten since lunch the day before and neither had
Breea. I felt painfully detached from anything that
used to be normal or real—as if I were watching from
a distance, disassociated and disconnected from everything around me.

As soon as we pulled into the bank parking lot, I
caught sight of my employee, Maria. At my captor's
command, I made a hand gesture to Maria that indicated I was going out for a cup of coffee. I always
made fresh coffee in the office for my staff in the
mornings, so I hoped Maria might notice the change in
my habitual behavior.

I circled the block a few times. Maria got the front
door open and went inside the bank with another of
my employees who had arrived to assist in the comple-
tion of daily opening procedures.

"Park in your usual place, the first one next to the
street," the talker ordered.

I pulled into my spot and parked. As I exited the
Jeep, the masked man threw me my briefcase and
whispered loudly, "Hurry the fuck up! And no phone
calls. We can see you from here."

He pointed to his pocket where the dreaded detonator lay in wait. In my mind's eye, I saw Breea sitting on the floor of her closet, her fragile young body lying on top of her little pairs of shoes, her arms wrapped around her knees. Then I saw her exploding into a million pieces if I failed in the task ahead of me. I sucked in a deep breath of cool morning air and exhaled with resolve. I knew what I had to do.

I opened the door to the bank and walked in. The click of my heels on the floor was all I could hear. I forced a casual smile toward Maria and Lorraine who were busy with morning deadlines. We all had a deadline in the morning, getting ready for the upcoming day of receiving and paying out monies. Today, I had an additional deadline as Breea's voice echoed in my mind, "You're going to do everything right Mommy. I know you will. Be brave Mommy . . ."

The dynamite pressed into my back as I walked robotically straight to my work area, laboring to breathe normally under the pressure of the tape digging into my ribs. I placed my briefcase on the floor on the left side of my desk. Then I sat down and opened the top right-hand drawer. There it was. The business card that read "On the Spot Photography by Christopher Butler."

Yesterday morning, he had been just another potential customer. This morning, he lay crouched in the back of my Jeep outside the door, holding the lives of my daughter and Allison and me in his pocket, while he waited to get rich. I imagined scribbling a note to someone, making a phone call, somehow alerting someone. Anyone. I picked up the phone to call my voice mail out of habit and immediately hung up shaking in terror, waiting to explode all over the bank. What if he thought I was calling the cops? I swallowed hard and straightened in my chair. They had Breea. That was their power—the only thing that would make me go through with this. They may have been evil, lecherous, and mean, but they sure as hell weren't stupid.

My stomach pretzeled into a maze of knots as I shut the drawer. I gazed at the photo of Breea on my desk, turning my head to look at another photo of us together. There was no man in either of the pictures. Christopher Butler must have noticed that. Never did I imagine that having a photo of my daughter and me on my desk would make us a target. I see now that they'd found me to be an easy mark, a single mother with a young daughter and no man for protection. The fact that I was personable, telling him that I enjoyed photography, and lightly engaging in a conversation also had been a factor. It may have been good for building business relationships, but at what price?

I felt tears trying to push through but I stopped them. The last thing I needed was for my staff to see me crying when I was trying to be invisible. I took a deep breath, kissed the picture of my little girl and reluctantly put it down. Then I relocated my briefcase strategically near the vault as I made my way to the operations area of the building. This way I could make my move without drawing attention to myself when the dreaded time was upon me.

A new teller for the day, a substitute from another branch, approached me. I couldn't tell the new girl that she wouldn't be there for long that day. As soon as I had my daughter safe in my arms, I would be alerting the authorities—if I were still alive. Either way, I knew that the bank would be closing for the day to investigate what I was about to do, whether I made it or not. "It's going to be an interesting day," was all I said as I showed her where to keep her lunch and which computer she'd be using. *Bad timing for her*, I thought. *Worse for me.*

In my mind I rehearsed my next move, filling the gym bag with cash. But what if Brink's didn't deliver the usual amount today? I "casually" checked the mobile vault that we called the "cash cow," where we kept a small amount of cash for the tellers' convenience. There was a pile of hundreds in there and I placed them where I could grab them as we went into the vault. Everything had to run as smooth as silk since the gunmen had given me all of five minutes to fill the bag, get out of the bank, and get back to my car. The leader's words echoed in my head, "You better get it all or we'll come back and kill you." I needed to make sure there were no delays or surprises.

I watched the clock. I'd never realized how jerky the minute hand was. It didn't sweep smoothly, but twitched spastically from one minute into the next. I heard the Brink's truck. Through the front windows, I saw the boxy gray armored truck cross the parking lot and drive to the back of the bank. I glanced at poor, unsuspecting Maria, mother of an infant. I hated that I was about to drag her into my misfortune, but I had no choice. If she did exactly what I asked, there would be no repercussions for her. But if she indicated in any way that something was not right or if she tipped off anyone, we could all die in a heartbeat.

A few minutes later, the Brink's truck retraced its route across the bank parking lot and out into the street. They had made their delivery. This was it! "Maria," I said as calmly as I could, "can you come with me a second?" I gestured toward the vault. As she got up to accompany me, I grabbed my briefcase, opened the door to the cash cow, and scooped up the hundreds. Together we entered the vault.

I closed the door and turned to face my employee. "Maria, listen to me, and don't say anything," I whispered. I quickly and quietly filled her in, lifting my shirt to show her the dynamite. Her wide eyes told me she wanted to bolt but I impressed upon her that Breea's life lay in the balance. I had her check the mechanism on my back for clues or numbers, but there were none. Apparently, my captors had done their homework.

Then, as if she suddenly had awakened to what was going on, Maria blurted out, "Oh my God, Michelle, you're robbing the bank."

Oh no . . . the microphone! Did they just hear that? I wondered what it felt like to blow up. Would it hurt?

Would I know they had pressed the button an instant before the explosives detonated? Was my angel in a million pieces already?

"I only have five minutes," I told her.

As I blankly watched my own hand reach for the cash, a vague sense of shame nagged at me. I stacked bundles of money denominations into the bag. Maria stood beside me, shocked and stuck in her place, unable to move. I made her promise not to call the police until I was well away, convincing her they had a scanner that could pick up police calls. At least that was what they'd told me and they were definitely calling the shots. My hand felt like it belonged to someone else as I continued to grab piles of money and filled the bag to the brim.

"Go out there and help the customers," I told Maria, "and get ready to close the bank as soon as I call. Then you can alert the police and corporate security. Come on Maria," I said, as she stood there in a semiparalyzed state. "You can do this. I'll call you as soon as Breea and I are safe."

We walked out of the vault together and locked it behind us. The first thing I heard was an employee yelling, "Michelle, I need your help. This new computer system keeps locking up and . . ."

"I trust you to take care of it. Call technical services," I called back to her as I bolstered the wide strap of the heavy bag on my shoulder past a line of customers waiting for a teller. The clock on the wall ticked to 9:01 AM. Someone who knew me tried to chat with me on my way out. "Off to an early meeting?" she said.

"Not exactly," I muttered as I headed for my Jeep. I opened the driver's side door and hurled the gym bag with all my strength onto the passenger's seat before getting in. The talker, still crouched on the floor in the backseat, instructed me to drive to the street next to Domino's pizza. When we passed a particular cul-de-sac, he pointed and said, "Your Jeep will be right here. Find your way back here to your car after I drop you off and then you drive straight home. No cops until 11:00 AM. Got it? Now drive into that parking area of those apartments and park in number eleven."

I did as he ordered but neither of us knew that the cops already had been notified. The moment I left the bank, Maria told Lorraine what had happened and she had dialed 911, told them I'd robbed the bank after being held hostage all night and they were en route to the bank, on the lookout for my red Jeep and me, suspicious about my involvement.

"Get out." Butler grabbed the bag of cash, his watery eyes glowing with greed. "Walk slowly." He let out that low, dark sound that was meant to be laughter. I got out of the Jeep and stepped onto the black tar, moving backward away from the gunman and my car. He climbed over the center console and into the driver's seat, shoved the shift lever in reverse, and backed out of the stall. He sped away.

I was alone. He had told me he would remove the dynamite when he got the money, but I was still wired to explode. What would happen next? Would they kill me now that they had what they wanted? Was the talker waiting for me to get into my car again before he detonated the dynamite? Or would they shoot us when I got home? Maybe the other men had already taken Breea. Or murdered her. Images of my dead child tormented me.

My step sped up as I walked to my car. I couldn't move slowly, no matter how hard I tried. I noticed a strange man, all alone, getting out of one car and into another. He was watching me. Was he assigned to kill me once I was on my own? I darted my head toward the cul-de-sac just in time to see a car speeding away from where my Jeep was supposed to be. It was copper colored, with louvers in the back window and a back end that looked like an old Nissan Z28.

There was my Jeep, the engine running, right where the gunman had said it would be. And I was alive! I jumped into the car, grabbed a pen. For lack of paper, on the gray vinyl passenger seat I jotted down the license plate numbers and descriptions of both cars I'd just seen. Then I drove home like a race car driver, the dynamite still strapped to my sore back that was surely turning black and blue. I gripped the wheel, my daughter's name echoing as I passed the bank, and flew up the streets of my neighborhood to our driveway—Breea!

ALLISON's Jeep was not in the driveway. Where was she and where was Breea? The men promised they both would be here unharmed if I got them the money. I wondered how I could have been stupid enough to believe them.

"God please . . . please, I beg you, let her be alive!" I mumbled as I rushed to the front door, which had been barricaded with a chair. With inhuman strength I pushed my way in and opened my mouth to scream for my daughter. No sound came out until the third try.

"Hello! Hello! Breea! Allison!"

"We're back here!"

How can I describe the relief when I heard Allison's voice answering me? She had said "we." My knees started to buckle, but I caught myself. I rushed into the bedroom to find Allison sitting up on her daughter's bed where I had last seen her. Half the tape was off her mouth, a strand of hair was stuck in her eyes, her hands and feet were still bound. I rushed by her to the open closet. Breea was there with her legs and mouth taped. I pulled her out, found a pair of scissors and freed her.

While Breea and I freed Allison, she explained that Breea had got up and walked into the living room and announced she wanted her mommy. They'd taped her mouth and legs and shoved her back in, leaving the closet door open. When Allison was sure they'd left, she'd convinced Breea to hop over and attempt to free her. They were working to free each other until I showed up. When Breea heard the door open, she'd panicked and hopped back into the closet.

We ran into the living room where I had last seen the gunmen, the dynamite still taped to me. All I wanted was to hold my little girl and I hadn't even thought that wearing the dynamite was endangering my child and my friend. Allison convinced me she could take the dynamite off of me.

"What if it goes off?" I said.

"I don't think it will. They ripped it off us like it was no danger to them at all. I bet they aren't even wired to explode."

"Okay, okay. Gently. Just get it off of me, get it off me!" I said, still terrified I would blow up at any minute. She began to cut the explosives off my back. Allison untaped me and she placed all the explosives outside at the top of the stone retaining wall that surrounded our garden. We couldn't make phone calls because our phones had been stripped of their batteries. I kicked off my black high-heeled shoes and we all ran up the hill toward the neighbor's house, paranoid that the men were watching us. I ran hunched over with Breea in front of me, ready to hear the sharp sound of gunfire, but we reached our neighbor's security gate, breathless and alive. My back throbbed where the explosives had cut into me. Frantically, I pushed the tiny black intercom button over and over, alert for strange men rushing at us from nowhere. From anywhere.

"Help!" I screamed into the intercom.

Someone finally answered, "Who is it?"

"It's your neighbors," I cried into the black box. "We were kidnapped all night. Please open up." The gate creaked and slowly rolled open.

At the top of the hill, my neighbor, Rick, stood in

his dark green robe, hands in his pockets, looking worried. We ran up the steep driveway and reached him, gasping for breath. I was babbling. "Please help us. Please. We've been held hostage all night. Three men, there were three. And there was a woman on the walkie-talkie. It was Lisa. I recognized her voice. The men had on masks and guns and they taped us with bombs and they made me take money from the vault. Call 911. I have to call the bank. I have to tell them to close the doors. I have to tell them about the man that was at my desk, the business card . . ."

I was rambling on and on, talking as fast as I could. Breea lifted her shirt to show the neighbor we weren't kidding. When I saw the remnants of tape still attached to her skin, I could feel myself beginning to fall down. I couldn't stop myself. My lids were closing as my neighbor reached for me.

"Mommy!" I heard from far, far away.

I blacked out.

5. Under Suspicion

THE room spun, the sounds were distant. Someone was calling my name but I was having trouble answering. I have no idea how I got from the driveway to the sofa inside the house. All I could mutter was, "Breea . . . Breea. Where is Breea?" I grabbed onto my daughter, who was standing in front of me looking confused and pale. I locked my arms around her until someone put a phone in my hand. I struggled to figure out who was on the other end of the line. Words suddenly took form, like the pieces of a jigsaw puzzle fitting together. It was my operations manager at the bank.

I squeaked out a sound. Then I found my voice. "It's me, it's me," I said. Then I started to scream, "Call 911! Lock the doors. Call corporate security!" I was suddenly barking orders into the phone. "Cover my desk and tell the FBI to take the business card in my top right-hand drawer, the one that says 'On the Spot Photography by Christopher Butler.' We're at a neighbor's house. Don't forget to cover my desk with something." I knew there were fresh fingerprints from yesterday, left by the man, Chris, with the hideous eyes beneath the mask. Lisa's fingerprints would be there, too.

The doorbell rang and Breea and I both jumped. FBI agents and detectives spilled through the door. The enormous speculation surrounding the crime combined with my position at the bank fed into a "possible inside job" mentality. This kind of investigator's mind-set ruined any chance of our getting help at the scene and there would be no fair treatment from the moment they stepped through the door of our neighbor's house in their dark suits.

Strangers surrounded us, drilling me with questions, but I kept feeling my face hit the floor and the ringleader bombarding me with questions just hours prior. It took me a minute to realize I was being questioned and I tried to answer but I must have sounded like a babbling idiot. "They said they were going out of town," I said. "You have to get them. Send someone to the airport. They said they were leaving!"

"Who said they were leaving?" an investigator asked.

"Them," I answered with mounting frustration. He was not listening to me. "The people who did this to us. They came into my bank yesterday afternoon.

They're the same people. His business card is in my desk. Please catch them before they get away!" They didn't appear to believe me.

I recalled distinctly that Lisa had said, "We're leaving town tomorrow and when we get our settlement, we want to make sure we have everything in place."

Holding Breea was all I wanted to do, but the nightmare continued as they gently took her from me and walked her into another room. "We need to take your statement," they explained, "and she can't be with you."

I watched my daughter slowly being led away, her sweet face turned to me in concern. Strangers were separating us again. I spiraled downward into a bleak, hopeless inner void while I tried to tell my story. The group of men in suits and ties standing around me looked ten feet tall in my traumatized state. The faces of the two female agents looked hard-bitten and unsympathetic.

They were nothing but faces to me as I rocked my body back and forth involuntarily on the couch of my neighbor's home, trying to explain what had happened. My mind would not follow a thought clearly from start to finish so I bumbled my way through visions with strobelike intensity that hurt my brain. I was having trouble staying in the present long enough to answer a question so I stood and paced. I sat down again because I felt sick to my stomach.

They continued drilling me. Why didn't they just go away and find the criminals who might be in

Mexico by now with a small fortune that I'd stolen for them? *They* were the criminals, the ones who deserved to be grilled like this. Would a crisis team or paramedics arrive soon—someone who could take care of us? We'd been abused, terrified, thrown to the ground, and wired with explosives that threatened our lives. Didn't that qualify as a crisis or trauma or shock?

No team, no ambulance, no paramedics ever arrived. Was it because our wounds were invisible? No blood, no help. Was that it? But we were bleeding to death emotionally.

I was stunned to suddenly see my boss from the bank, Brad, standing over me. Two male agents had pulled up chairs near me and Brad sat down beside them. Their constant questions were painful and I could still feel the barrel of an invisible gun making my temples throb. My wrists were painfully sore, as if they were still taped. I was in no state for this. Couldn't it wait until I felt better? All I needed—all I wanted—was some sleep, with Breea in my arms and someone we trusted watching over us.

"How many were there?" I heard that question as if from the other side of the room. Hadn't I already answered that one four or five times? Were they trying to trip me up? Didn't they understand that I was one of the good guys? When I opened my mouth to speak, I could smell the stench of the masked man, as if he were standing over me. I also saw my daughter, lying on the floor of the closet, her hands and wrists bound, the dynamite strapped to her back, her clothing hanging on the rod above her head. I couldn't decipher the present from the past. I saw Breea and me in the bathroom, being watched while we undressed to shower. They had been watching us for months. Was somebody watching right now? My eyes darted toward the windows.

Breea told me that Brad was taking her out for a hamburger. Was that wise? I didn't think so, but before I could voice my concern, she was gone. I let go. Everything was moving too quickly for me to find my place in any of it. I was no longer part of anything real or familiar and my "bubble" existence had begun, a state of trauma and shock that would never depart altogether. The questions droned on and all I could think of was Breea and why she'd been gone so long. It seemed like hours had passed when she finally entered the door with a Burger King bag. Brad guided her toward me with his hand gently at her back as they passed by me and into the back room, where I couldn't see or hear her.

At one point I wandered out to the back of my neighbor's home. A large pool surrounded by a wire fence overlooked our house below. Yellow police tape, shining in the sunlight, encircled our yard. A bomb squad hovered over the dynamite sticks on the retaining wall, taking precautions in case they were wired. I stared at it all, detached, with no connection to that house any longer. I watched camera crews and police activity buzzing around the house that was no longer my home. I would never live there again.

A cool wind blew across my face, making my skin tingle as I felt profoundly small in that moment and completely alone. What would we do next? Where would we go? How would I pay the bills? Was I going certifiably crazy with flashbacks that kept coming? Or was this the way anyone would feel in a situation like this? Had there ever been a situation like this? Would Breea be okay or would she become a shell of the child I had worked so hard to raise with self-worth? Would I ever recover and feel normal again? What *was* normal? When would someone show up to help us?

My neighbor brought out a large gray flannel shirt, which he wrapped around my shoulders. I must have been shivering. His mouth was moving, he was obviously talking to me, but I heard nothing. I continued to stare down the hill. I couldn't believe this wasn't a show I was watching. It was my life.

Fʀᴏᴍ where I stood, I could see reporters were already gathering with their camera crews. They had white vans with a crane sticking out of the side that lifted them in a cab high over the scene, snapping pictures from above. On the ground, at least twenty-five people milled around the reflective yellow tape, picking up objects, writing things down, and staring at the ground in crouched positions. They had to be looking for footprints and they were sure to find them.

At the far end of the yard, the bomb squad and evidence collectors suited up in thick metallic-colored gear and went to work investigating the explosive devices that had scarred our backs, permanently. I could see that they were inching toward them with great caution at first, but soon enough, a bomb squad special agent reached out his hand, picked up the device, and examined it more closely until he removed his helmet. Clearly, there was no danger and, maybe, as far as the dynamite was concerned, there never was. But that didn't make our ordeal any less frightening. In a sense, I thought with the little brain power I had left, it made no difference to the validity of what they had told us. We had believed what they said, because we had to, and we would suffer as badly as if the bombs had been real.

"Is anyone coming soon to help us?" I asked one of the FBI agents who had been interrogating me. "An ambulance or anyone to check us for shock or a trauma? You know, a crisis person?" I could barely speak.

"I don't know ma'am," the agent said as he led me back into the house so he and his buddies could get back to asking me their unrelenting questions. Breea ran up to me and as we held each other, I found out that her dad Jeff had called and so had Kristi, my best friend of seventeen years.

"Turn on the news, Kristi," a friend had told her over the phone. In horror, my best friend was riveted to her TV, as the words "breaking news" flashed across the screen. Just above it were images of my house with my Jeep in the background. Jeff, on the other hand, had been driving in the area in his work truck and spotted the commotion. They had made attempts to talk to us, so why had I not been allowed to speak to either of them?

I really needed Kristi, my soul sister, right then, whom I'd met while Jeff was doing a six-month stint in the navy. A simple hello one morning when we were both checking our mail had matured into a friendship of a lifetime. And then, Breea could have used positive words from her dad but it hadn't happened. It was one more emotional blow as Breea and I were both spiraling deeper into trauma. We were supposedly the victims here, not the perpetrators, but the strangers gathered here were cutting us off from family and friends. I wasn't even allowed to see Allison, who had been separated from us.

When I saw Allison's parents running into a back room to be with her, it became clear to me—I was under suspicion. Isolation hung over me like stalactites in a cave, frozen in space and time—until I noticed it was dark. The investigators were finished, thank God, and they informed us that we were free to leave. That sounded great but where would we go? There was no way we were sleeping in a house that had been destroyed by evil. But we had to get some of our things.

When I asked for an escort to go pick up a few necessities, two FBI agents walked Breea and me down the hill to our house of horrors. Breea waited outside and I have to say that walking back inside that house was a task that I still don't know how I accomplished. I must have been in shock as I walked past the couch, the kitchen where strangers had eaten my food, the bedroom where a masked man had watched me sleep, and the bathroom where lustful eyes had watched Breea and me take off our clothes, go to the bathroom, and take a shower.

I was maneuvering ghosts in the house. I grabbed some clothing and underwear and a few toys for Breea and headed back outside as fast as my legs could carry me.

When we stepped back outside, one of my employees, Lorraine, was waiting for me. I hugged her and then my boss, Brad, walked up to me, handing me a set of car keys. He'd gotten me a rental car since my Jeep had been confiscated as part of the crime scene. I appreciated the thoughtful gesture but how could I possibly drive? I was humiliated that my boss was witnessing me like this, falling apart, sobbing, too afraid to take the wheel.

Why are you handing me these keys? I wanted to scream out. *I can't drive a car. I need help. Can't anybody see that?* But I remained silent. I took the keys and put Breea into the car, where she curled up on the floor near the passenger seat, afraid of being a target. "Mommy, I feel sick." she said.

Exhausted and terrified, I started up the ignition in disbelief that anyone was allowing me to drive in my current state. The criminals were still out there somewhere and no one was stopping me. No one offered to help or to come along with us to protect us. *Please, run up to the car and offer to come with us, offer to help, please . . . please. Anybody,* I thought, as I began to roll down the driveway. My heart and head were pounding and my mouth began to water. I was going to throw up.

People disappeared from my rearview mirror as I headed to a hotel address scribbled on a piece of paper. In the fifteen minutes it took to get there, I pulled over twice, barely managing to get the car door open before I vomited. Headlights blinded my stinging eyes, cars flew past me like bullets as I gripped the steering wheel, trying to get us to safety, wherever that was. It was dark and I realized that just twenty-four hours ago, we had been attacked. Darkness meant something different now. Didn't anyone get that? Breea and I should have been given an armed guard or at least another adult, to escort us. But since there was no one but me, I drove like a zombie to a strange bed in the dark of night on the worst day of my life.

I pulled into a hotel driveway and rang the bell at the registration desk as the shrill sound mixed with other strange sounds in my head. The night clerk appeared. "Oh, Michelle. I heard what happened to you," she said. A young girl with narrow hips and sun-streaked hair dangling around her jawline, she had kind eyes and a gentle voice. *Thank God.* The security gate at the entrance to the parking lot had helped a little, too. At least there was a guard watching over things while we parked.

A bellman escorted us to our room, which to my dismay was located all the way in the back, as far from the security gate as possible, in the darkest corner of the property. I guess they figured we needed some quiet. The bellman looked at me strangely when I asked him to go inside and make sure nobody was there. But he indulged each of my requests as he looked under the bed, in the closet, in the bathroom. When he announced that the coast was clear, he left shaking his head. He must have felt sorry for us.

Nice of him, but pity was the last thing we needed. We needed protection, plain and simple, but it seemed like no one was taking this as seriously as we were. They would have if it had happened to them, but I could barely open my mouth to say as much. I hated that we were all over the six o'clock news. What if the criminals found out where we were and came to finish us off?

Breea wandered to a corner of the room where she sat on the floor, her arms wrapped around her knees, her back bent forward, her eyes tightly closed. I sat beside her, took her onto my lap and rocked her until she drifted off to sleep. Now I was alone with nothing but my thoughts. I slid a pillow under Breea's head and let her sleep on the carpet while I brought over the phone to call my best friend and brother, Dave.

Dave had my mother's bright Irish eyes, the color of the sea on a sunny day. His reddish hair, tending to-

ward strawberry blond, belied his gentle demeanor. I
wished I could cry on his broad shoulders and feel his
quiet confidence. He tried to ask me questions when I
reached him, but nothing he said was making any
sense. I could barely speak and Dave had no idea of
the magnitude of the crime or the amount of trauma
we'd suffered. He and I had been kind of distant for so
many years now, I wasn't sure who he was anymore.
He didn't know much about me either, but that was
about to change.

Then I called Kristi, who became hysterical when
she heard my voice. "I saw it on the news and I've
been trying to find you," she blurted out. "Are you all
right?" She repeated her question several times but
nothing was registering in my mind. I was fading, confused as to how to tell my best friend that, no, I wasn't
all right, I was in shambles. I hung up rather than try
to speak the words I could not say.

Breea awakened suddenly and started to cry, holding her tummy. I ran to her and we stayed on the floor
in the corner as I wondered how on earth we could
take back the pieces of our lives and fit them together
again. But just like Humpty Dumpty, it would take
more than the king's horses and men to make us
whole.

Breea fell into a fitful sleep while my paranoia escalated by the moment. I paced by the window, peering out through the shades every few minutes. My
heightened sense of alertness picked up strange
sounds like a creak in the floorboards or the wind in

the trees, and telegraphed them to my brain for analysis. Feelings I could not explain welled up inside me. Was there a way to get help? What should I ask for? What was really wrong with me? We were supposedly out of danger now, but I almost felt worse than when we were tied up on the couch. In fact, the freedom escalated my anxiety. I felt as if an evil force was about to come flying in from nowhere to eat up what was left of my daughter's and my sanity.

I rested on the floor with Breea. When the sun came up, I realized that I'd gone forty-eight hours with no sleep at all. I couldn't remember if I'd eaten or not. When the phone rang, I nearly jumped onto the ceiling, but picked it up with a trembling hand. Brad was on the line.

"Michelle," he said, "you're going to get a call from a woman named Eleanor. You met her during your training. Two years ago, she and her family were taken hostage at her home, just like you and Breea. I think she might be able to help you."

I hung up the phone. Eleanor had been a manager of another branch in my area before I was hired. She would understand what had happened to us. It had happened to her, too, and she still worked for the bank. That was hopeful. Maybe one day I could get back to work.

Eleanor called almost immediately, but her voice sounded anxious. "You're going to need a long time to recover," she warned. "Lots of time."

That made me feel worse. How would I feed my

child while we were recovering? Did she have any advice about that?

Eleanor rattled on about "taking the time you need to recover." From what I was able to glean from our conversation, she had gone right back to work until a full-blown nervous breakdown two years after the incident had forced her finally to deal with the trauma she had stifled for so long. I wondered how long it would take me to recover? And what about Breea, a seven-year-old girl? No one knew. I doubted my employer would be willing to let my job wait indefinitely until I felt ready to return to life.

By the time I hung up the phone with Eleanor, a woman who was supposed to help me, I felt desperate. I cringed at the sound of children outside our hotel window, popping balloons, the cracking noises reminding me of gunshots. I started packing up our things. I simply could not sit in this hotel room one minute longer. When I begged for a room closer to the security gate, the receptionist muttered that it wasn't safe to be anywhere anymore. Just what I needed to hear! Breea and I moved to another room where I hoped we'd feel better, but there was no such place. We were too afraid to go to eat so we ordered room service and prayed.

Three hotel rooms, three days, and three nearly sleepless nights later, Thanksgiving arrived. It was the first in a season of holidays Breea and I would have to get through somehow. Our first stop was at my ex-husband's house. Jeff s new live-in girlfriend and her family treated us like celebrities for being on the news. "How gross and twisted people are," I thought to myself, staring blankly at the buffet of holiday treats with no desire to eat.

By the time we left and made our way to Kristi's, I could hardly move except to constantly scratch at my crawling skin, dig at my scalp, and quickly move away from the direction of noises around me. I tried to control it. I couldn't. I felt like a complete nut job, but I couldn't help it. I was a mess.

We hung out in Kristi's kitchen, our favorite place to catch up on each other's lives over a cup of coffee or a glass of red wine. I felt like my body was actually somewhere else and at one point, I picked up the newspaper to scan apartment rentals. I could never go back to that house filled with ghosts of "them." But when Kristi joined in and tried to help me, I abandoned the newspaper immediately, shut my eyes, and clamped my hands over my ears to block out her voice. I could not tolerate suggestions. My mind interpreted them as pressure to find a new place to live, pressure to do what someone else was ordering me to do.

Kristi felt paralyzed, afraid of saying or doing anything for me. After seventeen years, our relationship was changing and there was nothing either of us could do about it. She wanted to offer that Breea and I move in with her, but she had a new baby and feared for her family's safety. After all, we had been stalked for months. She had no training in dealing with her best friend being shattered into a million pieces. None of us knew anything about the emotional aftermath of violent crime and I remember Kristi staring at me in disbelief, longing to connect and shocked to see what I was becoming. She wanted so much to reach Breea and me, but there was no way to build a bridge.

After a warm meal at her house, I heard a TV reporter announcing a fifty-thousand-dollar reward for information leading to the capture of the criminals in my case. I ran into the living room to see the screen. My employer was offering the reward. There were shots of our old house, my Jeep, and the yellow taped-off area that was labeled as the crime scene. The gunmen were still at large and why hadn't I heard about a reward? I'd told the authorities about the business card in my drawer right away. I'd described his eyes and his voice and the female voice on the walkie-talkie. I should get at least part of that reward to help us get back on our feet as soon as Christopher Butler was caught.

Suddenly, my eyelids became unbearably heavy. I fought to stay standing just long enough to slowly back away from the television. I caught myself before I fell and Kristi led me to the couch to lie down. Breea was in another room; I could hear her childish voice. Amid the sounds of people eating, drinking, and chatting calmly, I sensed that I didn't fit in anywhere anymore as I drifted into oblivion. I just couldn't fight it any longer. I was drowning with no idea how to save myself.

6. Beyond the Yellow Line

THE FBI clearly didn't believe my version of the story, letting me know, though they appreciated my detailed recollection, they could not build a case on my memory or the fact that I'd identified one of the men and the woman on the two-way radio. They needed hard, forensic physical evidence with no mistakes. That, I understood but I did not agree that the business card in my top right-hand drawer was too easy. They evaluated it as too stupid of a mistake for any criminal to make, especially gangsters like these who had gone to great lengths to plan everything to a tee. Soon enough, though, the FBI would find out that these criminals had made one big mistake after another.

The card in my desk produced a name, an address, and, after further analysis by the San Diego County

Sheriff's Department crime scene lab, a fingerprint.
The next step was to run a complete background check
on Christopher Butler. He had a long rap sheet and
was a convicted bank robber from Atlanta, Georgia,
recently released and on parole. With a sense of urgency, the FBI called in a covert multiunit gang and
drug task force led by Detective Rudy Zamora and Jeff
Higgins. God bless these men, who, from day one, took
on our case with gusto. They simply would not rest
until those responsible for this crime were apprehended.

At this point, the forensic investigation was in
progress. I learned that the team of agents and the
Evidence Response Team led by Detective Barry
Vechionni, had meticulously numbered fragments of
our destroyed life that they found in the house and the
bank. They knew that masked thugs wearing gloves
had ambushed us. And yet, gloves or no gloves, they
also knew that most criminals leave behind small,
sometimes infinitesimal pieces of themselves at a
crime scene. This was how they gathered and formed
evidence.

While the FBI interviewed bank tellers, other
agents were at the house, taping off the area surrounding the bomb and defusing the suspicious explosive
device. The sticks had sat on the stone retaining
wall—the torture instruments that had dug into my
back leaving me with the kind of scars you cannot see.
As a technician inched closer and closer to the device,
carefully positioning himself on the opposite side of
the wall, it had become clear to him that the device had

no timer. The graininess or marbling that appeared to be made from wood had alerted the bomb squad special agent that it was not real. He reached out his hand, picked up the device, and examined it more closely.

The wires were colors you would expect to see on dynamite sticks: yellow, black, and red. The center was carefully crafted to look like a wireless detonation device. The color, a deep brick red, was a perfect color to scare the hell out of unsuspecting victims. But the device was a fake, consisting of a wooden dowel cut in half, spray painted, and taped with rolls of pennies wrapped in black electrical tape with colored wires protruding from the center to the ends.

The crew of crime scene investigators scoured the property for clues while a sketch artist documented where each piece of evidence was found. The first big break was discovered in the dirt surrounding our house, where footprints led to and from the building. With a storm on the horizon, they had to move quickly to capture the prints before rain destroyed any chance of retrieving them from the ground.

A casting material the consistency of pancake batter was mixed and poured into the impression, hardening into a piece of usable evidence. They had one shot to get it right because even one bubble would render the cast of the impression useless. A matching pair of boots or shoes would be significant evidence linking someone to the crime scene where expert photographers snapped several technical shots of the prints.

Pieces of used duct tape had been discarded

throughout the house. They found blonde human hair stuck to them, which proved the traumatic violent experience we had undergone. The best news was that although the criminals wore gloves, they didn't cover their foot tracks. According to crime-scene experts, the most overlooked evidence contained within a crime scene is footwear evidence. A pattern that reveals scratches or scuffs can act like a fingerprint with very identifiable characteristics.

With latex-covered hands, the electrostatic dust print collector shone a special light on the slick tile floors, revealing thirteen invaluable prints—exactly what Barry Vechionni was hoping for. After that, a thin layer of dust on the smooth surface of the bathroom floor was lifted with precision. Both in the bank and at home, tweezer-shaped instruments put pieces of evidence in plastic Ziploc baggies. At one point a pair of expert eyes picked up a single black, coarse human hair from behind the driver's seat of my jeep.

Lastly, they vacuumed the house thoroughly and sorted through the contents, looking for clothing fibers, dog hair, foreign particles, and anything else that would lead them to these bastards. The investigators had learned through questioning "snitches" and poring over the crime scene that this was a gang-run activity. These days, forensic task forces with state-of-the-art technology were making it virtually impossible for crooks to commit crimes without getting caught. And still, they needed suspects. Detective Zamora needed to get Butler and Ramirez in his line of sight.

Word of the kidnapping and bank heist had already hit the streets and the detective and his team began to trace Christopher Butler's and Lisa Ramirez's every move. It seemed that the duo had taken off for Atlanta the day after the crime. Plainclothes cops, briefed by the deputy district attorney in the "war room," followed their leads to a dingy, roach- and drug-infested gang house on Avery Street. The twosome had paid cash for their last-minute airline tickets but they made a huge mistake when they stuck ten thousand dollars in cash under the pillow of their babysitter, Cassandra Stokes, who knew all about the heist. After leaving a safe that held a large portion of their cut in Cassandra's possession, they took off to Atlanta. Another mistake. When the babysitter called to report that the safe had been stolen from her apartment, Butler and Ramirez were holed up in a cheap motel contemplating their next move.

In the meantime, Huggins, the six foot four, 240-pound thug, had gathered his friends and blown a big chunk of his portion of the loot in Las Vegas.

Bones (whose name I later learned was Robert Ortiz), the last of the threesome, apparently had walked down the street with his dog, the money over his shoulder in a knapsack, and had disappeared.

By the sixth day into the investigation, my boss had upped the reward money for any information leading to the criminals. Around-the-clock surveillance of all the suspects began and, during that time, phone records were gathered as the criminals kept spending the money and a mountain of circumstantial evidence was piling up.

Greedy informants came out of the woodwork with information, ratting out their three buddies who apparently had loose lips and so much pride in their plan that they couldn't keep it to themselves. The investigators now had the real names of those involved and they knew that Huggins, who had had little formal trouble with the law, and "Bones" had Cripps gang ties.

They also knew that Bones was a violent criminal with a long rap sheet.

On the eighth day, it was determined that one of the wooden dowels used for the fake explosive devices had revealed an astonishing piece of evidence—a fingerprint left in the paint from an impatient mastermind. Their first attempt to reveal any fingerprints via heating and steaming superglue into a mist that stuck to paint had failed. They tried another rarely used technique, their last hope. Since the print was on a curved surface, it was difficult to capture and process for identification, but the careful application of a Microsil epoxy material, smeared on like paste, did the trick. The print was lifted, transferred to a flat surface, and processed for a match. The reward flashed across the computer screen: Christopher Butler.

With a search warrant in hand, the team of investigators organized a multiple location, simultaneous raid at 7:00 AM on November 29, 2000. When the SWAT team entered the motel room in San Diego where Butler and Ramirez were supposedly staying, the room was empty. Heading to the house on Avery, they knocked on the door.

A thirteen-year-old "wannabe rapper and part-time pimpette" named Princess answered the door. "What the fuck do you want?" was her greeting.

The detectives looked at the decrepit girl and had a moment of compassion. This pathetic creature was living in a garage with Huggins, aka Big Hershey. They soon found out that Butler and Ramirez lived in the living room with Lisa's unfortunate three children while various unsavory characters arrived there randomly to crash and score drugs. The floor was strewn with used drug paraphernalia, garbage, soiled diapers, and a smell of desperation similar to the worst kind of body odor. With Butler and Ramirez nowhere to be found, the police put out an APB on Butler's car. But the house was a hotbed of evidence.

In a bathroom trash can, a ski mask was found with eyeholes cut into it. Wires in the top of a closet were the exact colors of the wires taped on the fake explosives. In the closet was a pair of boots. Finally, in the back of the house surrounded by filth and waste, were a piece of glass with red spray paint that outlined the void of several objects, the dowels, and a can of spray paint.

When four police cars surrounded Butler and Ramirez's car at a stoplight as they headed south on Calle Jules within an hour of the raid on Avery, and officers with guns drawn and screaming, "Step out of the car with your hands up," they surrendered. In the trunk was a gold mine of incriminating physical evidence; a black duffel bag filled with empty bank cash wrappers, money straps, credit cards, and other stolen items belonging to Allison and me, black gloves, black nylon pants, and in the glove compartment, a loaded handgun.

The babysitter was taken in for questioning while Big Hershey was surrounded at a tiny motel in Paris, California, and arrested without incident. He still had some of his heist with him, but most of it had been spent. Bones had changed his name and skipped the state.

The boot prints lifted from our house matched the boots found in the closet, placing them at the scene. Carefully analyzed for color and chemical compound, the paint from the dowels matched the spray paint can and paint on the glass found at the Avery Street house. The dowels were also an identical match to the outline on the glass found during the initial raid. But the biggest and most valuable piece of evidence of all was the fingerprint belonging to Christopher Butler imbedded in the paint on the circular dowel.

Although the evidence was stacking up—the thirteen electrostatic dust prints matching the boots found in Butler's closet; the paint on the plate in Butler's backyard matching the chemical compound of the dowels—there were wrinkles in the case already. Because Butler and Ramirez wore the same size shoe, Butler never flinched during his interrogation, claiming informants were out to get him. As a result, he never admitted any involvement in the crime.

And while the forensic evidence should have foolproofed the case against the suspects, it didn't. Only a mere fraction of what is pieced together to prosecute criminals ever makes it into admissible evidence, and this case was no exception. Although Lisa Ramirez and Huggins made complete confessions, Lisa made a shocking claim (untrue of course) that she had heard me laughing and flirting with my tormentors over the two-way radio. Between that and the desperate informants wanting a piece of the reward, rumors began to surface that the kidnapping had been a ruse. The investigators began asking themselves, "Was the bank manager involved?"

And getting me into the cold interrogation room alone, and traumatizing me further, became an item on the FBI's "To-Do" list.

7. When Knives Talk

"PRETEND it never happened."

I stared in disbelief at the bony counselor, dwarfed by her large pink cushy chair in her plush carpeted office. It had been five days since the crime and Breea and I were hoping she could help us.

"Pretend your door was made of steel," she said, "and they couldn't break it down." She leaned toward me and smiled somewhat nervously. Her mousy dark hair was severely pulled back into a bun at the nape of her neck. Her thin lips matched the tiny arches of eyebrows she'd painted above her soulless gray eyes. "You see?" she said smiling again without involving her face, "just pretend it never happened." She performed a flourishing gesture with her hands.

"But it did happen, Mommy," Breea said softly. She

was sitting on the carpet at the other side of the office, playing with a LEGO set.

"Yes, baby, it did," I said defiantly, wondering how this woman managed to get a license to counsel anyone. She had been recommended by Brad but she was only making us feel worse. Five days after the crime I needed a qualified trauma therapist, not a family and marriage counselor. We had needed someone at the scene and since then, our trauma was compounding daily.

It seemed that Breea and I were suffering a variety of symptoms that neither of us could control or understand. We thought we were being followed most of the time, we both suffered constant stomachaches, and Breea insisted on riding on the floor instead of in the seat of the car. I'd hidden behind bushes more than once during those days. I'd even run out of the Super Saver one afternoon, leaving my groceries behind, certain I'd spotted Christopher Butler in one of the aisles, wearing his ugly mask. The worst part was that previously normal sounds now jangled my nerves. Loud television shows and the crashing of garbage trucks early in the mornings strained my nervous system beyond belief.

I saw right away that this woman disguised as a counselor had no idea what we were going through. I took Breea's hand and we left, both of us crying all the way to the car and back to our latest hotel room. By the time Dave, my brother, showed up at the hotel, we were emotionally destroyed, unable to make decisions or take any sort of action.

By day my boss started broaching the "back to work" topic. I knew the pressure wasn't coming from Brad himself. He was getting heat from his superiors, which was obvious from his sensitive voice and obvious struggle to discuss it with me. From a bottom-line business perspective, I understood. They wanted their results-oriented, turn any failing branch around employee back. But where was his bosses' humanity? Had they even considered what to do for a seven-year-old girl whose life had been shattered? I wanted to tell Brad that I would return to work when I could get into the car without trembling or imagining a masked gunman in the backseat or when I could sleep through the night without gruesome nightmares.

A victim of post-traumatic stress disorder, I relived the events over and over again in scrupulous detail. I could feel the dynamite sticking into my back and smell the duct tape pinching my wrists. It had been no consolation at all to learn that the explosives weren't real. We had thought they were and had suffered the terrorizing threat of instant annihilation. That didn't go away with an explanation. The horror that my daughter, Allison, and I might be blown to bits was as indelibly etched in my cellular memory as if the dynamite had been real. And so, in a sense, it *was* real.

The sickening dreams too kept coming.

I'm walking down the street and snakes begin to appear—lots of them surrounding me until I can't move.

Suddenly I'm grabbed by my feet and taken to a strange house against my will. I'm kept there for days with other girls also being held. There are no doors in the filthy bathrooms. I can't get away because of the snakes covering the ground and barbed wire surrounding the property.

I try to flag down a sheriff. He laughs and keeps driving. Then I find a phone and try to call my mom. I'm crying uncontrollably, asking her why I'm being held for ransom. She says nothing. The energy is frantic, as I search for a way past the snakes. I awaken crying, begging for a way out of the place where I seem to be trapped forever.

When I told Dave my dream, that I hadn't slept for more than an hour or two in the last several days, he insisted that both Breea and I get a massage to help us sleep. This, I agreed, would be a great way to immediately deal with the negativity now attached to anyone touching us. I was already thinking about ways to begin the healing process.

The masseuse was a kindly woman who helped get some of the kinks out of our sleep-deprived, tense bodies. The relief, however, was momentary, transient, and fragile. The same demons arrived with the sunset and so did the noises and agitation that would not allow me to drop into sorely needed slumber.

Dave helped more than he will ever know when he began speaking to my boss, Brad, for me. I simply could not cope with my mounting stress when Brad talked about my returning to work and I gained new appreciation of my brother's emotional depth and his capacity for empathy. I kept imagining my health insurance being canceled, which it was, and telling the lien holder to come tow my Jeep away. I couldn't drive it anymore with a ghost in the backseat, and I didn't care what it might do to my credit. I wanted it gone.

My fears escalated whenever my boss called. I harbored a secret fear that I would never again be able to work, that I would never be normal again, and that Breea and I would be separated when I could no longer care for her. I just couldn't fathom how life would ever get better with no career, no home, no car—nothing. On top of that, the FBI had become regular visitors as they kept asking me the same questions. It took me several of their visits to realize I had not been ruled out as a suspect in the bank robbery. Hadn't Breea's and my paranoia clued them in? Apparently not. Not only was I being denied the help and consideration that a victim of a violent crime needs so desperately, I was also under a constant shroud of suspicion.

One afternoon my father showed up at the hotel with a bouquet of flowers. He told me he had hired a PI to track me down. It may have been a heartfelt gesture, but his unexpected visit triggered a resurgence of my turbulent childhood. He'd been so angry for most of my life, he reminded me of the men who had kept me hostage. Actually, though, I owed him a big thankyou. If he hadn't been so selfish and abusive while I was growing up, I never would have known how to handle the gunmen. Being my father's daughter had taught me how to deal with others' irrational behavior. He had trained me to walk on eggshells and avoid breakage—the technique I used with my kidnappers.

I remembered that once my father traded in the family car for a three-wheeler motorcycle that revved loudly enough to satisfy his ego. When he had extra cash, Dad bought an expensive leather jacket to enhance his image while we walked around in our secondhand clothes. On rainy days, I was devastated that we were made to wear green plastic trash bags with holes cut for our heads and arms, as he drove us around town, showing off on his "I'm so cool" machine.

I didn't trust him back then and I still didn't trust him when he tried to say something to comfort me. I'd wanted to hear those words all my life, and now it was too late. I was too wounded to care as I listened with half an ear. I questioned his motives concerning the visit, wanting to believe it was all about love. But I suspected he liked the chaos and hoopla, along with the press that would single him out as my father. In fact, his visit caused me so much stress, I was relieved when he left. It was not the time to sort through the rubble of my past. Not yet.

I was not relieved, however, when my brother Dave left. I understood he had to return to his life with his son, Shawn, in Los Angeles, but I was forlorn without him. I watched him drive away late one evening, leaving me to face the dark shadows climbing over the balcony. No matter how many people told me differently, I could not shake the belief that someone somewhere was lying in wait to attack us. Poor little Breea had spoken barely a word in days and we held on to each other tightly each night when we went to bed. I rocked her to sleep, unsuccessfully trying to sleep beside her, afraid to lose my tenuous grip on both of our lives.

I made the following journal entry at 4:00 AM:

December 10, 2000

I miss Charlie, our dog. I miss my life before they took it away. Breea is getting worse. Scared of doors and windows now. She said she could hear one hundred doors slamming in her head last night. When will it end? I see THEM on the balcony, climbing over, scaring me. I better go to bed and hold Breea. I wish we weren't alone.

The ringing telephone jolted me early one morning. I jumped up to answer it, finding the concierge at the other end of the line. We were checking out that day and he wanted to know what time we'd be leaving. I'd found an apartment-style hotel in which I could cook our meals. It was located near the beach, a familiar place. It seemed right for us, so we moved in.

Brad, my boss, paid the rent for the next three weeks and I felt completely out of place. True, I had a small kitchen where I could cook, and maybe return to a slight sense of normalcy, and we could take walks on the crowded streets. But my plan to reintroduce myself to the world at large backfired.

One afternoon, when I went to the local Warehouse Store to buy some music, a clerk saw my name on my credit card.

"You're the one from that bank robbery, aren't you?" he said. "You're staying here at the Carlsbad Inn, right? That's such a trip, what happened to you I mean."

I grabbed my credit card and ran out of the store, leaving the CDs behind. If this guy knew who I was and where I was staying, the criminals could find us in a second. I rushed back to the inn, locked the sliding doors, and stared into the mirror. "Why?" I asked myself. There were no answers.

I threw off all my clothes and stared at the puffy dark circles beneath my eyes. Permanent lines on my forehead had popped up overnight, aging me well beyond my years. I didn't recognize myself. All I could see was a frightened woman, stripped naked, both inside and out, struggling to stay conscious. I was losing my grip and I had no idea what to do. I climbed in bed and pulled the covers up.

I wrote the following journal entry early in the morning of December 18, 2000:

I woke up with a heavy head. So much to think about. The meeting with the prosecution team is today. I feel extra jumpy and the nightmares were worse last night. I awoke without breath. I sat straight up and I was shaking. Sounds behind me

*make me cry. My eyes still look crazy but I look okay.
I did my hair nice for the first time and got new
shoes. That feels good. There's too much in my head.
I'm so confused. Breea's voice is medicine.*

After nine long days and horrifying nights, the attempts of my friends and family to get me to socialize were proving unsuccessful. Kristi tried renting a funny movie, one with Renée Zellweger called *Nurse Betty*. We popped popcorn and pretended it was a regular home movie night. But I shrunk into the couch when a scene showed Zellweger with duct tape around her wrists and ankles. It was still too real for me.

By the time the FBI arrived to escort Breea and me to Children's Hospital's Chadwick Center for the videotaping of her testimony, I was struggling with an ever-thickening bubble of mistrust. It only got worse when I was made to wait outside while they took my traumatized daughter into a private room with a therapist I'd never met. They also refused to allow me to watch Breea through the two-way mirror adjoining the room.

I stood in the hallway, feeling helpless, hunched over at the waist and curled up one moment, frantically pacing the next. A woman with reddish hair and a kind face approached me.

"Are you all right?"

"No, no. They took her away from me again. They took her." I mumbled as I sat crouched with my back up against the wall of the hallway. I was rocking back and forth, my arms wrapped around my knees.

"Come with me. Come on." She gently guided me into an office and invited me to sit on a comfortable leather chair. I was scratching my skin, passing my fingers roughly through my hair and rocking back and forth, side to side, unable to speak.

The woman picked up a phone. "This is Iby Kantor, I have a woman in here who needs help," she told someone on the other end of the line. "Get the psychologist here immediately with medication for anxiety."

Then she knelt down in front of me and softly said, "Tell me what happened to you."

So there *were* angels among the monsters. I whimpered and said, "I don't know. I don't know what happened to me. I don't know what's happening to me now. It's all a big mess and I don't know what to do. Everyone keeps taking her away from me. Everything is gone . . . everything is gone . . ." I was completely dismantled.

The angelic woman gently repeated her request for me to tell her what happened. I tried to control my hands from kneading my hair as I started to speak about the crime to someone without judgments for the first time. She made a follow-up call for the anti-anxiety medication. "Can you get someone down here with crime victim paperwork too?" she said. "No, no one has helped her in nine days. I know it's ridiculous. She and her little daughter are the victims of a heinous crime; you know the story of the bank manager from the news? Yeah, well that's them. Bring the minor forms as well. Thank you."

I knew with certainty, that just like the couple in the van that night so long ago, I could trust this woman. She wanted me to feel better and although my personal hell was still alive and well, suddenly I was not alone. I took the pill that was handed to me, waiting for a half hour until the medication began to do its soothing work on me. Within an hour, I was calmer than I'd been in days. When they returned Breea to me, I took her back to the hotel armed with sleeping pills and a slight softening in my heart, a faint glimmer of hope.

December 14, 2000

I need some answers from a good attorney to find out more about my rights. I put the punching bag back up and I can't wait to put on my headphones and beat the shit out of it like it was them, tied up in a closet with explosives on their backs. How could they look at my sweet little girl and do this to us? I keep needing to pull over to the side of the road while I'm driving and vomit.

I now know HATE. God, please help me!

I was picked up in front of my hotel by an unmarked government car the next morning, under the guise of bringing me in to review evidence. A man with an open face and an easygoing manner introduced himself as Joe Barend, the deputy district attorney assigned to prosecute the suspects in our case for the State of California. Apparently, he'd been at our neighbor's house that evening after the incident, but I didn't remember him. He seemed nice enough, his short beard and mustache making him look distinguished and his ready smile encouraging—when he wasn't hurling painful and repetitive questions at me. Barend was supposed to be on *my* side of the law, but when he escorted me into a white-walled room with a few hard-backed chairs and a lone table, it was clear he had other loyalties.

I looked at the people gathered for my questioning, a number of whom would be my daily companions when the trial began. Diane, assistant to Joe and the only female on the team, was slim with long dark hair, olive skin, and intelligent eyes. Detective Rudy Zamora was a stocky Latino man, sharp-witted and approachable. Dale was older, a typical undercover, rough biker-looking guy with deep-set eyes and yet something gentle about him. Finally, Detective Jeff Higgins finished the team, a clean-shaven, conservative-looking man who was well-dressed, handsome, intense, and attentive.

The meeting had supposedly been called so we could all get to know each other and review the evidence. So why did the process feel abusive? Why did Barend bombard me with probing questions that had absolutely nothing to do with the kidnapping or the robbery. They came faster than I could answer them:

"Tell us everyone you slept with in the last three years."

"What happened to your marriage?"

"Did it break up because of your sex life?"

"Was it because you were a stripper?"

"How much money do you have?"

"Did you ever lend money to your lovers?"

"Why are you doing this?" I yelled. "So what if I bounced a check once or if I took off my clothes a hundred years ago to get through school? I'm the first person to file bankruptcy after a divorce? Why are you doing this to me? Stop it, please . . ." My voice faded as I dropped my head into my hands.

"We're just doing our job, Michelle," said Higgins. "They said you were in on it and we need to . . ."

My head shot up. "Who said I was in on it?" I demanded.

"One of the suspects. The woman. She said you were part of it in her confession. The others confessed too, except for Butler, but she's the only one who mentioned your name." Ruby looked me square in the eye. "Were you involved in this bank robbery?"

The walls began to sway. I jumped up, knocking my chair to the floor in my haste, unwilling to control my outburst. "For you people to insinuate that I would ever have anything to do with harming a single cell of my daughter's being," I informed them, "is insane. Suggesting I had anything to do with criminal activity is more than disgusting and if you don't point me in the direction of bathroom, I'll vomit on you right here and now."

I rushed out of the room and down the hall to the

ladies' room. I flew into a stall and dropped to my knees, sobbing and vomiting into the toilet bowl. Sweating profusely, I stood slowly on wobbly legs, pressing my arms against the walls of the stall to steady myself. I wiped my mouth with toilet paper, then with my sleeve, and left the stall to stand in front of the sink. I looked in the mirror at the only person who would really listen to me. What had happened to the corporate go-getter, the woman who loved her job as bank manager and felt proud to have made her life work for herself and her daughter? Just when it seemed like it couldn't possibly get any worse, it had.

I splashed some cold water on my face, wiped it off with a scratchy paper towel, and returned to the "interrogation" room. The system that was supposed to help me was turning on me instead. I looked each of the men and the woman in the eye, my voice slowly rising in pitch and decibel level as I spoke. "If you people think I had something to do with this mess that ruined my own life, it's absurd! I'm not perfect and, yeah, I may have done some things in my life that I'm not proud of. But I'm not a criminal and my daughter is my world, so stop this line of questioning now!"

"Hey, Michelle," Zamora said. "We believe you. We're on your side. We just have to do this to rule you out."

Tell me another one, I said to myself, hardening my heart. If they were on my side, they had a funny way of showing it. On the way back to my hotel room, I wondered if there was a difference between the good guys and the bad guys. They were all starting to blend together with their blindsiding tactics and questions that were none of their business. My list of "The People I Can Trust" was diminishing by the second.

I wrote in my journal that night:

December 18, 2000
Even home feels like a locked prison. So many locks and I still hear and see them inside. Maybe time will diminish these feelings. Breea is still wetting her pants, curling up in a ball a lot, scared to go potty. I wish I could make it all go away for her. My heart is in a million pieces.

I was asked by the prosecution team to return to the old house to relive the worst experience of my life, this time with cameras rolling and the prosecution team surrounding me. They were going to take Allison's statement, too, to help the prosecutors build their case, and I suspected they were checking to see if our stories matched. Even with our tormentors in custody except for Bones, I was still a suspect in the robbery, it seemed, something that stunned and upset me almost as much as the crime itself.

I phoned Dave, unable to face reentering the scene of my terror without my brother. He drove in from Los Angeles, picked me up at my hotel, and we headed for my old house.

I was trembling when we drove up the driveway for the first time since our ordeal. The FBI agents were already there and a wave of sadness swept over me as I looked out at the view. Ghosts of Breea and Allison's kids on the old swing set tormented me as I walked along the front yard. I braced myself as I entered the empty house, but nothing could have prepared me for the nuclear blast of agony that hit me in the stomach. I stumbled from room to empty room (the contents of the house were in storage now thanks to Allison), trying to show the agents as much as I could in vivid detail. Dave stood by me, struggling to keep his composure as I visibly became more and more shaken reliving our pain and suffering.

When I got to the bedroom where they'd forced Breea into the closet, I lost control. I staggered at the doorway and grabbed onto the jamb to steady myself.

"Are you all right, Michelle?" Dave asked. "Can you do this?"

I nodded.

"Are you sure? We can come back."

I was sure. I wanted to get this over with so I could leave and never return to the memories. They were all still there—the men on the sofa, their dog, the smell of marijuana, the pounding rap music—locked in my memory, frozen in time, replaying over and over. The watery, bulging eyes, the guns at my temples, Breea begging me not to leave. I suddenly rushed from the house and flew into the car. I'd had enough. The house on the hill was haunted and my flashbacks increased every day. I began to have severe suicidal thoughts that scared me. And although my will to live was strong, my desire for just one moment of peace in my mind was increasingly horrifying. I was afraid of my own tendencies. I had to bring myself back to the thought of Breea to keep me alive.

My greatest fear was the skinny man the FBI called Bones, his gang identity name. He was still at large and he knew everything about us, part of the reason I kept switching hotels. Luckily, Dave had arranged with Brad to continue paying for our room and board until January 3, 2001, while I was in the most desperate situation of my life. But each time I wanted to break down and scream for somebody to take care of me, I remembered how brave Breea had been that night. I tried to be there for her completely, dealing with my own pain and fear when she was asleep or in school.

As Christmas vacation approached, I dreaded the season that had always been my favorite, especially since Breea was born. I used to shake jingle bells, throw rocks on the roof to sound like the reindeer's hooves, and set up a camera to capture Breea's joy when she ran from her bedroom to the tree to see the gifts wrapped in colorful paper with great big bows. Our tradition was that after she saw the tree on Christmas Eve, she went back to bed and waited for morning to open her gifts. But this year, it took everything I had to face Christmas and the celebrations that accompanied it. I was certain that the crime couldn't steal the spirit of Christmas from us, but I was wrong.

Once again, it was Dave to the rescue. He and his thirteen-year-old son Shawn took Breea and me to the local Christmas tree lot. Breea loved Shawn, a long and lanky blond-haired, blue-eyed kid four years older than she. We got a small tree that we smuggled into our latest hotel room and we decorated it with a few drugstore ornaments. We placed small white lights over it and hung stockings on the wall with pushpins, determined we would have Christmas this year as usual, despite the way we both felt.

On Christmas Eve, Dave and Shawn joined us as I put the presents under the tree and set up the camera just like in years past. When everything was ready, Dave shook the jingle bells and we waited for Breea to run out from the bedroom of the hotel—but she didn't come. He and I looked at each other sadly as he shook the bells again. Still no Breea.

I went into her room to find her hiding under the covers of the bed we shared, shaking, crying, and holding her stomach. When I asked her to come out and see what Santa had left her, she wailed, "It isn't Santa, Mommy. It's the bad guys coming to get us."

My broken heart broke all over again. My daughter was afraid of Santa Claus. I gently talked her down and she followed me into the living room, clinging tightly to my leg, hiding behind my nightgown. She looked at the tree, at Dave, at Shawn, and at me. "I just want to sleep, Mommy." She ran back into the bedroom and dove under the covers.

On Christmas morning, we unwrapped our gifts, emptied the stockings, and headed to Kristi's for our traditional gift exchange with her family. By then I felt like a zombie, simply going through the motions. *Where is the joy?* I wondered as I watched Breea clutching her new doll to her chest far too tightly. Kristi gave me a bound journal to write in instead of the random pieces of paper I would grab or rip from Breea's *Winnie the Pooh* notebook. It was the perfect gift for me, but that night, Breea was holding her stomach again, feeling sick, and wanting only to sleep. I sobbed for her and for me, realizing how much had been stripped from our lives. Would we ever feel safe again? I feared we wouldn't, but one thing was for sure. Neither Breea nor I could begin to feel safe until Bones was behind bars.

8. Escaping from Wolves

My decision to get out of Dodge came on a warm night in June. We had been living in a cottage-style beach house for six months with bolted doors and windows and planks of wood sealing the window in the room Breea most feared, the bathroom. Our frazzled nerves were not helped by late-night beach-goers, and our desire to have a somewhat normal existence without being recognized by the man still on the loose led to a trip to the local Rite Aid for a bottle of dark auburn red hair tint. With my hair color success-fully changed and after watching Breea's golden locks hit the vinyl floor until the lobes of her ears were showing, we had begun to ride our bikes and check out the local cafés.

Tips, particularly one from an ex-girlfriend of the delinquent, had allowed the police to quickly surround him, lob tear gas into the building through the windows, and extract him from a small crawl space in the apartment complex. When he was finally apprehended and arrested, a compelling amount of evidence was collected. The local news said he was about to be extradited back to California to determine whether or not he would stand trial.

"I didn't do nuthin', man," he said as he was being escorted in handcuffs to a Wisconsin jail. Even though Ortiz was off the streets, my job of helping to put the case together for the prosecution wasn't finished. I was not pleased when I was asked to return to the *other* scene of the crime—the bank.

I went there with a new attorney and the entire prosecution team, including the DA, several FBI agents, two detectives from the sheriff's department, the gang task force, and my ex-boss. I wanted to assist the prosecution as much as possible, but reenacting the events of that horrible day while they audiotaped my testimony ignited the trauma that was always smoldering just below the surface of my skin.

The bank felt like a morgue, with death threatening at every turn. My career dreams and hopes had ended in this place. I remembered being in a trance the last time I was there. I trudged through the motions, showing the team my old desk, stopping for a moment to gently caress the shiny polished surface. It felt like another lifetime and, in truth, it was. When I stepped inside the vault, claustrophobia overwhelmed me. I couldn't get enough air into my lungs. I fell apart in there, dropping to my knees and sobbing as I relived reaching for the money and stuffing it in the bag. I explained through my tears how the dynamite had hurt my back. It was as if I could feel the duffel bag still lying heavily on my shoulders as I retraced the steps I took lugging the bag of money outside and into my car. Then I had to endure the retracing of the route Butler ordered me to take.

Two weeks later, the grand jury proceedings began.

This hearing allows the prosecution to present their case, evidence, and witnesses to a jury without the defense present. It would determine whether there was enough evidence to take the case straight to trail, without pretrial. My arrival at the courtroom for the grand jury proceedings remains a blur in my mind, but I recall the building as being sharply square and sterile and I was driven there in a black unmarked car by a plainclothes detective. When the detective took my arm and led me through security and up to the room for the hearing, I felt the old pangs of dissociation taking over—my built-in method of protecting myself and supervising the situation from above.

The pace of events slowed to a crawl as my heart sped up. Everything seemed to be moving backward and the invisible protective bubble I'd envisioned surrounding my body grew thicker by the minute. The bailiff opened the door for me, and I stepped reluctantly into the courtroom. It was windowless. Thank God the criminals were not at the hearing, I thought, because I was not ready to look into those horrific eyes.

The judge looked through me. I was simply a name on a docket to him, I suppose. A panel of strangers waited for me to explain one more time the events of the robbery. I slid into a chair that squeaked every time I adjusted my weight and the questions began. It was the basics at first: name (please spell it), address (please spell that, too), and the name of the financial institution where I had worked.

I rattled off the answers quickly, not having to think or feel until the judge said, "Ms. Renee, would you please tell us what happened to you on November 21, 2000, when you arrived home from work?"

I took a breath, uttered a silent prayer, and launched into my story, loath to repeat it again. I *had* to heal, that was what my life was about now. But reliving the misery over and over was not allowing that to happen. Still, I did my best, trying to get the words out without breaking down, until the proceedings were stopped abruptly. After some whispering, the bailiff left the room in a big hurry. I looked around, wondering what had happened. Had I done something wrong? I began to tremble when the investigator said, "Ms. Renee, we just received a call about a school situation."

"Oh my God," I moaned, "Breea!"

"No, it's not Breea," he assured me. "The bailiff's daughter is a student at a school where a shooting just occurred. We'll have to continue this another time."

I was distraught that I would have to come back

here again, but my heart ached for the bailiff. I knew the horror of a child being involved in a violent crime.

March 27, 2001

The wind was strong last night, making our home creak and groan. It made Breea so scared she couldn't sleep. "I hear the doors opening, Mommy," she whimpered. "My tummy hurts real bad and I can hear the robbers talking in my head." When I asked her what they were saying, it was "Let's go." She had heard them say that to me when Butler was taking me to rob the bank.

She and I walked to each door and window together, making sure they were all locked and sealed up tight. She wanted to sleep and so did I, but right after we both dozed off I was awakened by the sound in my head of Allison's screams from that night. I wonder what happened to her. The trial is right around the corner. How will Breea and I ever get through it?

One week later, we were back in court with a new bailiff. I never found out what happened to the previous one, but I had to concentrate on my testimony. I sat in the hard, repulsive chair for several hours and when it was over, it took the grand jury about five minutes to determine there was plenty of evidence on all twelve counts to go to the next phase. Two criminal trials would occur, two criminals at a time. It was the first win for my side, the good guys, but life did not get any easier.

Within a week a phone call from the prosecuting DA took me by surprise. "Michelle," he said, "I don't want to alarm you but I need to make you aware that retaliation in cases like these is not uncommon. Firebombs have been hurled through the windows of some of the other witnesses—the gang members and others who testified against these people at the grand jury proceedings. We have to get them out of town and protect them. It isn't good."

"What are you saying?" I asked. "Are we in danger?" I heard myself whispering into the phone as if a third party were listening. "Do you think we'll be next?"

"I don't know," the DA said. "We have to run a complete risk analysis, which could take a while. At least a few weeks."

"A few weeks? What if I don't have weeks?" I pleaded with him. "What are we supposed to do in the meantime?" I heard the anger in my voice and apparently so did he.

"Listen, Michelle." He was using a soft voice, trying to calm me down. "I'd guess the risk rate is between ten and twenty percent. That really isn't high enough to put you in a formal witness protection program, but getting out of town wouldn't be a bad idea. We'll start the risk analysis and get back to you."

Right, I thought, *if we lived that long.* Christopher Butler had already tried to escape from jail once, I'd been told. I contacted Iby, my therapist, to tell her about the latest developments. She contacted an agency that assisted primarily domestic violence victims in these sorts of situations, and after conducting a quick assessment of our situation, they made the "helpful" suggestions that we move out of the state and change our names.

"Pick a new last name. Try to have fun with it," Sam from the agency had recommended.

Fun was simply not in the cards these days, especially for Breea. There was a preponderance of Latinos in her new school who pulled her hair (she was the only blonde in the class) and threw pebbles at her when she got off the bus. Her Latino teacher spoke mostly Spanish, leaving Breea unable to understand the material. I told my distraught little girl that my own school days hadn't been much better, when I didn't have a bedroom and I was too embarrassed to invite a friend over. What would my friends have thought about my sleeping on the couch and keeping my clothes in an old wooden dresser in the garage?

I explained to Breea how I'd felt in so many new schools where I was frightened of everyone, in agony from a home life that I didn't want anyone to know about, and I'd kept my head down. Breea didn't laugh when I told her I could identify every crack in the cement and the shoes each student wore, while their faces never looked familiar. She eventually made a few friends here and there, but I realized we had to find another school where she would fit in better. I was determined to do whatever it took to make life easier for her.

The trouble was that I had no money, no means to get any, and nowhere to go. But my decision was made for me as I approached our house on a late, dark evening. As I inched closer and closer to the premises, my stomach hollowed and my heart pounded. Men were casing the property. One of them was peering over the back fence, while another walked the perimeter, with the third standing guard near the garage. My anxiety jumped off the charts. It was the last straw.

We rushed to a nearby neighbor I had befriended, paralyzed with fear. After spending a sleepless night there, I called the DA in the morning. "I saw people casing our home last night," I told him. "Did you get that risk assessment yet?"

"Not yet," he said. "Unless your house is burned down or something similar, there isn't much we can do at this point."

"Are you saying our house has to burn down to get some help for us?" I shouted into the phone.

I still couldn't believe the DA had no real information on witness protection for me. He even had the nerve to say they would only take action if it were "an extreme case of aggravated intimidation."

"This isn't extreme enough?" I shrieked into the phone. I was outraged that something severe needed to happen before they would protect me. I'd watched a TV show in the past dealing with exactly what I was going through. It seemed that several state's witnesses were murdered before their trial date arrived. I wanted to blow the lid off my case, to expose the dangers in which we, the victims, were forced to face all alone, with no help from the authorities. It was no wonder our healing was going one-step forward, two steps back.

When I hung up, my next call was to Iby. I wanted to tell my therapist about what had happened and, although I wasn't sure where we were headed, Breea and I were as good as gone. No matter what the authorities were willing or unwilling to do, I couldn't risk sticking around. I made a few calls and, with some help from Breea's dad, within forty-eight hours I had purchased a round-trip ticket for Breea to fly to Alaska to spend three weeks of the summer vacation with Judy, her paternal grandmother.

I was tormented as I grabbed some of Breea's things and stuffed them into a small rolling suitcase decorated with sunflowers. I zipped it up tight and sat there a moment, watching Breea cry, assuring me between sobs that she refused to go anywhere without me. After all, we'd barely been separated for a few school hours since the break-in and I didn't like the idea of sending her away any better than she liked going. She was a seven-year-old child who had never flown by herself. This was a long flight; I should have been going with her, but where would I get the money for another ticket?

I exhaled, picked up the phone one last time and began to plead with Alaska Airlines for a deal. *If I can just get one person to understand*, I thought, *one per-*

son who will listen and help us. That one person was Becky, a ticket seller. "Hold on," she said after hearing my story. "I need to talk to my supervisor about this. Stay on the line, Michelle. Let's see what we can do."

Ten minutes later she'd gotten the okay from her supervisor to put me on a flight with Breea. All I had to pay were the taxes and airport fees. Breea stopped crying as I began to sob with relief. I threw together some clothes for myself and stuffed them into a bag. *Thank God*, was all I could mutter as I dozed off with Breea in bed beside me, ready to leave the city in the morning.

I didn't have time to arrange a ride to the airport so I decided to drive us and leave my car there, since I was scheduled to return home in four days. The plan was that I would get Breea settled, return home, and, soon, I would come back and find us a new place to live. Breea did not know that I'd be leaving so soon to close down our house (to avoid paying rent for another month) and I didn't tell her. When we passed through security, I was greatly relieved that Breea did not have to make this journey alone. I was getting her to safety and the rest simply didn't matter.

I love to fly. I adore being above the clouds, savoring the feeling of being between worlds, and the peace of clear blue skies. But this trip was not a peaceful one. I trusted no one at this time and sitting beside strangers made me feel like I was suffocating. I grabbed a napkin and began to write down some new last names for Breea and me. I was ready for a new identity. But what last name did I like? I wrote out several options: *"Fiore" (which means flower in Italian) is nice,* I thought. *Or maybe "D'Este," the name of my Italian ancestors.*

Nothing seemed right or natural. I was currently known as Michelle Ramskill, but I no longer wanted any part of the name I had when we were kidnapped, the name the criminals knew. I didn't want to use Estey either, my father's name, for obvious reasons. Finally, I decided to take my middle name, Renee, as my new last name and I scribbled my new signature over and over.

Then I reached for some travel games that a friend had given us as Breea and I decided on what to play first. We did it the way we decide a lot of things. We played rock, paper, scissors. I won. I chose to start with backgammon, and then we did a round of checkers. By the time Breea had settled into her Hello Kitty coloring book, I had put on headphones to listen to some music. I took Breea's little hand in mine and focused on the promise of beauty in the wide-open Alaskan wilderness where we were headed.

No sooner did we step off the plane than Breea's grandmother Judy, the ultimate safe space, embraced us. A tiny little thing with a friendly face and warm smile, Judy had such a sense of strength and presence that I exhaled deeply when Breea ran to hug her. Breea's aunt and two cousins were there too, and I nearly cried from relief as I was surrounded by familiar people whom both my daughter and I trusted. They asked us no heavy questions, just, how was the flight and were we hungry? I felt like a rag doll as I followed them to the car.

So this is the last frontier, I mused to myself, anxious to explore it as soon as I got some real sleep. I climbed into the car on jelly legs but when I rolled down the window and let the chilly, crisp air blow across my face, something inside of me began to wake up. And just like it was happening to me, the color seemed to be coming back into Breea's face and her eyes brightened.

I inhaled the air as if I were breathing for the first time. I wanted to kiss the earth as I tilted back my head, opened my mouth, and devoured the air as if I were drinking raindrops. The sound of a nearby rushing river lulled me as we passed brand-new green foliage bravely peeking up from the ground at the end of a long, bitterly cold winter. I felt as if I'd just come from the same place, one that was far behind me now. I imagined the budding foliage of my own life beginning to grow up around what had died that night in November. Alaska would be a place for Breea and me to heal, far from grand juries and investigations. My personal storm was on pause.

During the twenty-minute drive to Judy's house, we passed enormous trees, their branches reaching up and out in an embracing posture. Their flashes of bright jade and the colorful flowers bursting open reflected in the sun, transforming my black-and-white world into a rainbow of energy. When we pulled up to the two-story, four-bedroom house, a redwood cottage at the foot of a giant mountain, I knew we were exactly where we needed to be to start putting our broken pieces back together.

Judy had decorated the interior in a floral theme, with objects that held meaning from her past scattered around the house. I knew her things from when I'd been married to her son and I picked up a familiar picture of Jeff holding Breea when she was tiny. I'd taken that picture myself and it had always been one of my favorites. I smiled warmly, put it back in its place, and then strolled among the towering pine trees in the backyard, grateful that Judy's sweet spirit was welcoming us.

That night, Breea and I pulled down the dark green blinds to block out the blinding midnight sun of the summer solstice. We slept without fear for the first time in months. It was a great new beginning, as I wrote in my journal:

June 26, 2001
Hearing my inner voice for the first time in so long, it sounds like a stranger. Sleep comes easy here and for the first time since November 21, we slept with the door to our bedroom . . . wide open!

Four heavenly, ghost-free days passed in the Alaskan mountains. We slept well, ate well, and savored the pristine beauty of the frontier. When it was time to honor my ticket and return home to take care of unfinished business, I felt I could do it, now that

Breea was safely ensconced with family, far from the place where she had been traumatized. I really had no idea whether we should just move to Alaska and start our lives anew, or go back home and try to feel safe again. But whatever we finally decided, I had to go home and get everything out of that house so we could save the precious rent money.

On my last night, as I lay awake, restless and begging for some clarity, an inner whisper began to tug at the edges of my attention. It beckoned me, telling me that I needed to go back to our old life, give away most of our belongings, and drive back here to be with Breea where she was safe and sound. It sounded like punishment to leave Breea, fly home, and then to drive all alone across the United States and Canada to get back to her. But I'd learned to obey my inner promptings, the only guidance that consistently had led me in the right direction. At least, I could hear it again.

When I broke the news to Breea that I had to go back for a short time, she took it better than I'd expected. We agreed to concentrate on my coming back for her, but I felt enormous pain as we rode to the airport with Breea sitting in the back of Judy's car with me. I held my little girl's hand and peered at her face from time to time. She looked stoic, demonstrating a control way beyond her years. But as much as I admired her grit, I was distraught that she had to be so grown-up, so early in her young life. In fact, in that moment, I felt like the kid while Breea seemed wise beyond her years.

When we got out of the car and I was about to pass through security, I knelt down and gave Breea a big kiss and hug. My heart ached. Was I making a mistake by leaving her here? What if she fell apart the minute I left? What if *I* did?

Of course, Breea did not want me to leave, but she knew she was safe with her grandmother. So did I, which made our leave-taking less desperate than sad. It was July 3, 2001, five days after we'd arrived, one day after I'd heard the inner message, when I tearfully kissed Breea good-bye, locked pinkies, and promised I'd be back by July 15 to celebrate her eighth birthday. I tore myself away. At the gate I turned to see four little fingers moving up and down, reluctantly waving good-bye.

9. The Road Back to Her

I walked along the ramp to the plane, trying to quiet my mind. "What if she loses it? What if she gets sick and I can't get back to help her? What if she gets hurt and I can't be there to pick her up and put on her bandages?"

The questions went on and on and there were no answers. I boarded the plane, frustrated that I couldn't stop the evil in the world from harming my daughter. I hated that I had to even consider it. What had happened to us? Was I to blame for the trauma that plagued her now? Why couldn't I have seen that I was entering a dangerous profession and refused the position as bank manager? Was I just too busy to realize I was being stalked? Reeling with guilt, I staggered to my window seat, my throat feeling constricted. In thirteen days, Breea would be turning eight and how would I make her life work for her? How could I make our life normal again?

> *July 3, 2001*
> *I'm on the way home but I have no real home. I'm flying alone above Mt. St. Helens and although the sight is beautiful, it's hard to enjoy it knowing I won't see Breea again for two weeks. This is the longest we have ever been apart and my head feels heavy. I cried when I boarded the plane in Alaska and I can't wait to get back to her.*

I rested my head against the cold Plexiglas window and closed my eyes. I had no idea who was sitting on the seats beside me and I was too sad and confused to care. As the plane lifted off, I stared out over the magnificent snowcapped mountain peaks and gratefully, I drifted off to sleep for an hour or two.

The next day back in San Diego, I organized a front yard giveaway. It was a veritable sale of the century with a road trip donation jar for anyone who wanted to contribute to my imminent journey north. Hand-scribbled paper signs with the words "free" or "make me an offer" dangled from furniture, broken bikes, old clothing, and lamps in my front yard. It didn't take long for the crowds to arrive and swoop up my old stuff—things that I'd thought had meant something. They didn't. All that mattered was Breea and getting back to her. When the sale was over, I would be rid of everything I didn't want, need, or care about.

In the late afternoon, my sister arrived with her husband and their pickup truck, ready to store in their garage what hadn't sold, along with some sentimental things I could not part with—like the refurbished treasure chest that held my pregnancy diary, pictures of the sonogram, and the dress that Breea wore home from the hospital. I missed her so much as I stroked the beautiful blue dress trimmed with white lace in which she'd been wrapped when we first took her home. In just nine days, I'd be seeing her, smelling her hair, touching her soft pale cheeks, and kissing her with a lump of pure joy in my throat.

I was so anxious to get started back to Alaska, I decided to begin the trip right then and there—after I stopped in to see my landlady. I paid up what I owed and stuffed nearly five hundred dollars in my pocket, some from my security deposit, some from the donation jar. It wasn't much. *It has to be enough. It just has to be.*

I cleared the last food items out of the refrigerator and threw them in a white and blue mini cooler that was positioned perfectly on my backseat for easy access. Then I grabbed the canister of pepper spray I'd purchased weeks before and put a leash around the neck of Haley, my sister's pit bull, on loan for security. My work here was done, but my car already had 104,000 miles on it. What if it broke down? I'd be forced to seek help from strangers. That scared me more than anything else. But then, I had sweet-tempered Haley, who could turn into Fido the Ripper at a moment's notice.

I had one final call to make, to my brother Dave. He said he could hear my determination (he knew me well by then) and understood I was doing exactly what I needed to do—what I was being led to do. My final stop was at Kristi's house to tell her how much I loved her.

"Are you really going to do this?" she asked with concern showing on her face.

"I *have* to," I told her.

It was impossible for her to understand. As close as we were, she was my polar opposite—red-haired, more sophisticated than I could ever be, and definitely not the type to go it alone in life. She was married and she had placed "security" at the top of her list. She was high maintenance and she did her best to keep me grounded. I, on the other hand, brought out the deeper, more spiritual side of Kristi. We were more than friends. We were soul sisters.

"Well, you've always been a free spirit, Michelle," she said. "A real adventurer. I couldn't do it, that's for sure, but this is definitely you. Call me every day. You know I'll be worried sick." I loved it when I brought out that motherly overseer.

I hugged her tight and kissed her cheek. Buoyed by Kristi's good wishes, I hit the road to Alaska on July 6, 2001, as the sun was setting in the western sky. When she watched me drive away in the packed mini SUV, all alone, I can only imagine how worried she must have been. But I was doing what I had to.

I watched a magnificent sunset to my left and the

thought that the sooner I left, the sooner I could wrap my arms around my little girl kept replaying in my mind. I gripped the wheel, wiggled my body into place, and settled in for the long drive, nearly four thousand miles. I was overwhelmed by a sense of peace, a certainty that I was doing the right thing. I videotaped the place I had grown up in, the place where I gave birth to the most precious gift in my life, the place I used to love so much, San Diego, as I drove away, watching my broken dreams disappear in the rearview mirror as I headed north to the Interstate 5 freeway. Good-bye old home. Good-bye.

ALL the campsites were full when I arrived at Pismo Beach a little past midnight. I could smell the salt in the air and saw glimpses of twinkling lanterns in scattered places as I searched for an inexpensive motel or hotel. My problem was that no one would take in Haley, the pit bull. Inching along an arrow-painted road dimly lit by my parking lights, I crept up on a campsite by the beach, a little remote for my taste, but I had to sleep somewhere. My eyes wouldn't stay open much longer.

There was no guard at the gate as I drove through the entrance, looking for a spot to stop and try to blend in. I found a small empty area where I parked the car. After draping towels over the windows, I leaned my seat back and covered myself head to toe with a thick cotton blanket. I prayed and dropped into an exhausted sleep, the canister of pepper spray clutched in my hands and Haley curled up in the passenger seat.

A knock on the car window startled me awake in the morning. I reluctantly peered my head out from under the blanket to see the man whose campsite I'd borrowed. He looked stunned when he saw me, as though he'd expected anyone other than a young blonde and her dog. I slowly pushed aside the towel with the light stinging my eyes and I explained my plight. Thankfully, the kind man allowed me to stay at the edge of his paid-for campsite until I could pull myself together. He even offered to watch my stuff while I found a place to brush my teeth and hair. I hadn't trusted anyone in so long, I didn't know how to anymore. My mind was in a fierce battle, giving me simultaneous and opposite orders. It was between "You're ready to try" and "Run for your life."

Even in my terrified state, however, I recognized that the urge to run away had lived inside of me my whole life and it was about to change. I was on this trip for a reason and it had to have been divinely inspired. I took a deep breath, looked the strange man square in the eye and said, "That would be great. Thank you for your kindness."

I headed for the fifty-cent shower and washed my hair. A sense of freedom began to swell up in me as I rinsed the suds off my head. I was heading into another day on the road with more guts than the day before. Next stop, Napa Valley's wine country.

Every morning, every night, and every stop in between, I checked in with Breea on my cell phone while she kept track of my progress on a map that Judy had gotten for her. I drove toward the center of California, stopping in coffee shops and videotaping people I met along the way. The truth was that I was reveling in the unexpected discovery that I was free to be simply myself. There was no one to judge me, blame me, or see me as someone I was not. If they did, I was finally unconcerned because I was discovering a sense of luxury and calm in being alone with no one to worry about, protect, or impress. There was no one to convince and no more stern-looking suits and shiny shoes interrogating me as if I were a criminal. I knew that I needed strength to withstand the struggles ahead, the revictimization I kept hearing about. In my opinion, that is the brutality of the justice system when it comes to violent crime victims. And so, I needed this trip, guided by my instincts, to teach me how to function in the world once again, fear and all.

I sailed along Highway 1, the Pacific Coast Highway, a route that stretched from San Diego all the way to the farthest points north. Taking in the magnificent scenic seaside route with its glorious cliffs leading down to crashing waves, I stopped occasionally to enjoy the view. I kept telling myself that it was safe to get out of the car, although I didn't really believe it was. I have to admit how grateful I was to have Haley with me when I arrived in Napa well after dark.

I found a hotel quickly, but they would not take dogs. So I pulled into their lot, parked between two cars and put up my designer towel window blinds to catch a little shut-eye. Four hours later, I stirred and found the nearest coffee shop for a thick hearty cup of coffee and a warm, freshly baked blueberry muffin. Then I turned the music up, rolled my window down, and took the curves through the lush vineyards of Napa.

When I stopped to photograph the wineries that resembled Old Italian villas, I knew I was meeting myself for the first time on this trip. I was beginning to love the girl, the woman: unashamed, unapologetic, and unconditional. I set down my camera and lived out a fantasy I'd envisioned a thousand times. I took off my shoes and ran between long rows of vines that were waving in the breeze. Exhilarated, I danced, skipped, and twirled in the hot sun, letting go of my inhibitions. I hopped up on a wall made of large smooth stones and drew a self-portrait, which turned out vastly different than the rest of my artwork.

After so many dark, fear-based drawings, that day I'd drawn myself with a peaceful expression, lying on a blanket, resting. I named it *Sweet Dreams At Last*. Hope was slowly returning. *Tuscany must be so grand,* I thought, knowing in my heart that I would go to visit it someday.

I was in a really good mood by the time I jumped into my car, but as the sun rose higher in the sky, a scathing heat came with it. I broke out into a sweat and my car labored until the little black gauge hit the red zone on the dashboard. I pulled over and turned off the engine right away, something my ex-husband had taught me. He had been so good at taking care of our cars.

I sat under the shade of a towering eucalyptus tree while the engine cooled, thinking about Jeff. We'd taken several road trips together, back and forth from California to Washington State, but they were nothing like this. He never stopped to take in any scenery, but he'd made me laugh a lot, though, and he was easy on the eyes. Standing tall at six foot two, he was as handsome as a movie star and smart as a whip, but underneath it all, he was hiding major insecurities. In the end, he and I had turned out to be fundamentally different people with completely opposite goals. But when I met him, I'd been so mesmerized and in love, I'd gotten married too fast to find out whether or not we were compatible.

About an hour later, my car had cooled down enough to give it a nice, long drink. Haley and I got back in and hit the road again, as I felt strangely capable and in control. Several hours and a few towns later, I drove past the massive ancient trees in the Redwood forests of northern California. *Breea would have loved them*, I thought to myself. I stopped the car and walked across a thick tree stump, balancing my steps, my arms swaying back and forth like a tightrope walker, a smile turning the corners of my mouth upward. The sensation was unfamiliar since I hadn't smiled in a long time. I let the warm feelings fill me up. The little girl inside of me was emerging, ready to play, and I was positively thrilled to find her after all these years.

T HE sun would be setting in an hour or so, and I wanted to cross the Oregon border before it got dark. At 10 PM, I pulled into a gas station in a chilly downpour in Southern Oregon to get some gas and a cup of hot cocoa. But when I got back to the car to get in beside Haley, she leapt up and put her paw on the top of the lock with her nose pressed against the cold window. I was locked out. The keys dangled in the ignition, Haley's tail wagged a mile a minute, and I had to brave the rain again and run back into the minimart.

The attendant, a Middle Eastern man, spoke almost no English. Frustrated, I walked back outside into the soaking rain, terrified, seeing the bogeyman in the shadows, wondering what on earth to do. Three men walked out of the store, looking like they were returning from a fishing trip. I caught my breath, tried to stop my voice from shaking and asked for help. They responded immediately by calling the local fire department. Within ten minutes, a big red fire engine pulled up to rescue me from the massive downpour. The car door was opened in a jiffy and I thanked my rescuers profusely, got back in the car, and stared at Haley with anger.

I wanted to blame someone else for locking me out, but it wasn't Haley's fault. It was mine. I'd never really taken responsibility for the wrongs in my life. Instead, I was used to running away hoping my troubles wouldn't follow me. Of course, they always did—until now. Taking inventory was a new strategy, but it wasn't easy since I was viewing everything differently since the crime. Even things that seemed insignificant held life lessons, now that my eyes were wide open. I could see that if I hadn't been locked out of the car, I would not have needed to ask for help. This was number 2 on the list of lessons in trust and faith on the trip so far. Looking on the bright side of things took on a whole new meaning as the rain ferociously battered my car.

I drove away, rain loudly hitting the roof of the car, heading for any place that was dry and warm. Dead set against spending the night in the car in the rain, I ran in and out of hotel lobbies in search of a place with a cheap room that allowed dogs. I finally spotted a hotel sign that flickered neon red letters that read COZY ROOMS. I slowly approached the reception desk, the look on the bored clerk's face as dreary as his hotel. But when he quoted me thirty-five dollars a night and gave Haley a pat on the head, I paid in cash and took the empty room. I was not pleased that it was located at the end of the building, very close to the street, but after having slept in the car, the bed looked warm and inviting. I barricaded the door with a heavy wooden table and checked out the bathroom. A hot bath sounded like heaven.

I poured shampoo into the tub to make bubbles and I soaked luxuriously, thinking of Breea. Soon, we would be together again. I could feel my muscles unwinding, my back relaxing as I lay there in a trance, amazed that I had gotten this far. I needed to be strong, not only for myself, but for my daughter. What kind of role model can I be for her? I wondered. Had I ever considered my legacy to my daughter? What would it be?

I closed my eyes and thought back to a time when my own mom was going through emotional hell, lying in the hospital after yet another suicide attempt. I'd been sickened by seeing her bloated body after they'd pumped her stomach. Her eyes had looked dead and she seemed to be nothing but an empty shell.

"Mom, you need help," I'd said. "You need to be in a facility that can help you sort this out." I pleaded with her in front of the hospital as she sat curbside in a wheelchair with a few of my siblings nearby.

"No, I don't need help," she retorted. "I'm fine."

How could anyone think they were fine, five days after a suicide attempt?

She continued, "I'll just go back to work and forget about everything. Just get me back to my apartment."

"But Mom . . ."

"I don't want to talk about it anymore," she'd insisted. "Let's just go."

Did I do or say something wrong? Why was she so angry? As usual, I blamed myself. Even though we brought her home, she was destined for more hospital beds in her future, yet another reason to numb myself with drugs during my teenage years. Self-destruction was the food I'd devoured for so long, I'd convinced myself that God wanted nothing to do with me any longer. Why else would He have allowed my father to beat me and make me suffer so much? I'd felt like a teenage disgrace back then and before I knew it, I was listening to heavy metal music and taking the drugs that so often accompanies that lifestyle. What had happened to the times when my mom and I had laughed and danced together in the living room, blasting the music of Elvis, Barry Manilow, and Neil Diamond?

I dipped my head underwater in the tub and began to scrub my scalp. I would get through this and Breea would be proud of me. She would never turn to drugs because I was determined to show her a better way. I got out of the tub, dried off, put on my sweats, and set up the video camera. While my hair dried, I talked about the trip so far, imagining Breea watching the tape with me as I told her everything about my journey. Then, turning on my bedside lamp, I lay back on the pillows, pulled the covers over my head and fell into a somewhat peaceful sleep.

I awakened feeling optimistic and poured some milk from my cooler into a tiny box of Rice Krispies. Just before I was ready to get back on the road, I taped myself saying with a smile, "Let's go see what the day has in store." Unfortunately, though, I found out soon enough when I returned the key to the front desk, loaded my stuff in the car, and discovered that my left rear tire was flat. I waited for the old sinking feeling, but it didn't come. At least the tire hadn't blown out on the freeway or on a dark road in the middle of the nowhere. I grabbed Haley's leash and off we walked toward the center of town, a couple of blocks away.

Sure enough, after I turned a corner and walked halfway down the block, there was a gas station where I could roll the car. Thank God the street was on an incline, and it was lucky for me that I was pointing in the downward direction because hiring a tow truck would have blown my excruciatingly tight budget. As I rolled into the station, behold, a very cute guy in a blue mechanic's uniform greeted me.

While he went about fixing the tire with a permanent patch, I looked out to admire the view. There was a trail leading down to a rushing stream and as I began to follow it, I fell on my butt, laughing and bumping my way down. I landed at the edge of a magnificent waterfall beside an old brick wall overgrown with moss and curling vines. The water looked so clear and inviting, I wished I'd brought a bathing suit with me. But in the next moment, my clothes were off and I was splashing around in the water, naked as the day I was born.

When I got back in the car with the tire repaired, I realized I'd shredded a great deal of fear that day. I was about to start up the car when a pleasant looking couple walked over to the window. "Have you ever driven through Emerald Park?" they wanted to know.

"No," I replied. "It's a must-see spot. Take the time to see it. You won't regret it."

That particular national park had not been on my

itinerary but the next thing I knew I was making my way through a lush green forest. To my left was an unobstructed view of the ocean as the road passed old abandoned buildings overgrown with foliage. The winding roads created veritable treetop tunnels with people riding bikes or strolling alongside, holding hands. I stood on the edge of a cliff and imagined it was the edge of my new life, a moment I will never forget.

That evening, I pulled into a fifteen-dollar-a-night campsite on the edge of a sparkling lake. Sitting outside my car on a small lounge chair, I was approached by a lovely woman who said she managed the park. When she noticed I had no tent, she asked me where I intended to sleep. I pointed to the car. It took no convincing for her to talk me into driving with her to the sale at the local Kmart to purchase a tent. Within an hour, I had some shelter, the owner of the park had lent me her tent pad, and Haley and I were sitting in our dome-shaped temporary new home. I wrapped up the brand-new fold-up scooter I had brought for Breea's birthday. It was bright yellow and I knew she would love it. That night, I slept like a baby.

I awoke to the smell of eggs and bacon wafting from a café down the path. I couldn't afford to eat there, but fueled by a cup of steaming caffeine I was ready to speed through Washington State, determined to be in Canada by nightfall. I was making a beeline for the border but my heart stopped when I saw the sign for the Tacoma Bridge exit, heading toward

Seattle. I'd forgotten that driving by the place where Jeff and I had gotten married might affect me emotionally. My ex and I had first crossed this bridge together when the navy relocated him near Seattle. In love and dead broke, we'd settled in the small town of Port Orchard, Washington, where we dug up clams for dinner and used the heat from my blow-dryer to keep warm.

Jeff had proposed right after the move to Bremerton while we were standing on the dock, after he'd returned from a two-week trip at sea. Four days later, on January 22, 1988, I was a bride, wearing an inexpensive homemade dress. We exchanged borrowed rings for the ceremony, but I didn't care. Looking back, I wasn't so sure whether Jeff was ever truly in love with me.

We lasted seven years, a lot longer than it was healthy. I guess sometimes what we want is not meant to be because Jeff's drug use became so prevalent that I couldn't overlook it any longer. Divorce was something I had wanted to avoid, but couldn't.

The pain of it all hit me as I approached the bridge, trying to see through the tears that were spilling down my cheeks. "What is the matter with me?" I chastised myself. "It's been years. I'm fine . . . I'm fine." I straightened my back. I'd been too busy making a life, having a career, and being a single mom to truly feel much of anything about Jeff, let alone how much my failed marriage hurt me. But I was in my car alone now with nothing blocking my true feelings. I wasn't fine.

When I found a rest area, I stopped, grabbed my cell phone, and called Jeff. He picked up the phone right away and I told him everything I needed to say. He made a joke the way he usually did. "What's wrong with you? Don't make me do my Fire Marshall Bill impression." I tried to laugh. He did his impression.

"Ah, come on," he teased. "That was good. You gotta admit."

"That *was* good, Bub (the nickname I gave him when we were dating), but I'm hurting and I need to talk to you about something important."

Surprisingly, he didn't hang up. When he heard me blubbering, the woman who'd always been tough, strong, and independent, he knew something was up. "Are you okay? Where are you?" he asked.

"I am looking at the Tacoma Bridge sign," I said.

"Ohhh." He knew. "I can't believe you made it that far, but if I was driving, we'd be there already." He spoke with irony in his voice, but he was right. If he were driving, there would be next to no pit stops, and absolutely no streams or paths! That was Jeff, a no-nonsense kind of guy. I let out a giggle, in spite of myself.

"I could almost see the little white church we got married in," I told him, "and it all became real. We have never talked about how badly the divorce hurt me. I think I need to put this behind me and tell you how I feel."

"You're right," he said, to my amazement and relief. "It's time for that. I'm all ears, babe."

We talked for almost an hour, reminiscing about the good times. We laughed about the clams and cases of macaroni and cheese, the mattress on the floor, the firewood we had to pillage, and how hard we worked to get it right and make a good life for ourselves. Then we shared how we felt about our marriage falling apart. For the first time, I could tell he really was sorry for what had happened to us.

"I ruined the best thing that ever happened to me, Michelle. You. I can never say I'm sorry enough. I am so sorry."

Just before we hung up, I said, "I'll always love you, Jeff. I forgive you and I take responsibility for what I did wrong in our marriage."

I can't describe how different I felt after the talk. But when I started driving again, I recognized that this road trip was turning out to be more than getting from point A to point B. It was the road to recovery—not just from the horrible crime, but from life, from feeling broken, and from all the heartaches, lost dreams, and buried pain. Those were being replaced with something bigger and better that I didn't fully understand as yet. All I knew for sure was that I'd never felt so free from my past.

THE town called Hope in southern Canada was three hours from the U.S. border. I pulled into a nearly deserted campground and paid fifteen dollars for a big spot next to a retired couple who I soon discovered was traveling in their motor home for the summer. They welcomed me and took an immediate liking to Haley, a good sign. We chatted for a while and they invited me to join them for a hot meal. "We're cooking up some chicken," they said, "and there's more than enough. Why don't you join us?"

"A home-cooked meal would be amazing," I said with a big smile. Cans of tuna were becoming tasteless. "When do we eat?"

"How about six?"

"Perfect! I'll see you at the dinner table."

I ran off to take some pictures of a great old bridge I'd noticed on the way. I'd spotted a small white trailer parked there on a dirt lot by the edge of a river. An easel stood nearby with a straw hat hanging over its corner. It looked like a Norman Rockwell moment, an irresistible opportunity to shoot some film.

I jumped into the car with Haley and returned to the low wooden bridge, off of which five young boys were jumping into the water below. I clutched at my stomach for a quick second when I recalled that jumping off a bridge to my death, landing in the cool, deep waters below, had been one of my suicide plans. As the boys took turns jumping and applauding each other over and over, I thought about Breea. How would she feel if I'd gone ahead with my plans to end my life, and she had to watch my corpse being hauled out of the water? That would be the end for her. What on earth had I been thinking? Thank God I'd learned in my therapy sessions that I could replace negative thoughts or images with new ones. The therapist had taught me how to retrain my mind and this was a perfect opportunity to test the theory.

I parked the car and introduced myself to one of the young boys, a chubby kid who was too terrified to jump in. I tried to get him to go for it with me, but he refused. "If I can do it, so can you," I urged him.

He was dead set against it. Although he was friendly and encouraging when I told him I wanted to jump with his group of boys, I could see his self-esteem was suffering. "I bet you'd make a great cameraman," I said, offering him the camera. "I may never get this chance again, and I'm documenting my whole trip to Alaska."

He nodded enthusiastically. "Are you a movie person?" he asked.

"No," I said, "just a lady who needs to remember what it's like to be a kid."

I stood on the edge of the bridge holding hands with a bunch of boys. They couldn't believe a woman in her thirties was about to jump with them. "You sure you wanna do this, lady?" one of them asked.

"Yup. I'm positive."

Together we all counted, "One, two, three," and we leapt into the air. My fear evaporated midjump and I hit the freezing water, screaming with joy while the boys screamed right along with me. I was having a ball and I climbed back up on the bridge to do it again. "Race ya to the top." I said.

"You are too cool," one of them said as we clambered back up the bank for another leap. "I wish my mom was like you."

I hadn't heard the word "mom" in days. Breea would be proud of me. I was proud of me. I wished I could call her and tell her what had just happened, but my cell phone had stopped working after I crossed the border. The thing that was so astounding was that the moment I jumped, it was as if my negative visions and past suicidal thoughts flew away on the winds. I thanked the boys and when I got back in my car, they waved frantically and screamed, "Good-bye, good-bye!" They'd learned from me that you're never too old to be a kid again. I'd learned from them that you're never too old to grow up and face your fears head-on.

When I reached the white trailer, I snapped some great photos while I left the car running. But when I was through, it was déjà vu. I'd locked myself out of the car once more, and I hadn't heeded the firemen's advice to get an extra key made. Once again, Haley was locked inside and I was so angry at myself, I wanted to scream out loud. Instead, I went to the side of the road to flag down some help.

Within minutes, a young woman stopped her car and stepped out. She was about my age and she was wearing khaki pants, a T-shirt, and tennis shoes. A camera dangled from a strap around her neck. She was naturally pretty, the kind of woman who needs no makeup to radiate beauty.

I was still damp from my bridge-jumping adventure, which must have puzzled her. "My keys are locked inside my car," I told her. "All the windows are up, and my dog is in there. I just stopped to snap a few shots of that great scene over there by the river." I pointed to the easel.

"It caught my eye, too," she said, lifting the camera from her chest. "I'll go get some help. You can stay here with your dog." She extended her hand. "My name's Linda."

"That's my mom's name, too," I said. "I'm Michelle. That's Haley in the car."

"Great to meet you, Michelle. I'll be right back."

She drove off to find a phone and call a tow truck. By the time she got back, I was pacing and in a panic, worried about Haley locked in the car in the stifling heat. Linda's return relieved some of the pressure and kept me from breaking the window to save the dog. He looked okay even though he was panting a little bit. It wouldn't be much longer.

"Where are you headed?" Linda asked as I settled down to wait for the tow truck.

"I'm going to Anchorage, Alaska. My daughter is there, and I promised I would make it by her birthday on the fifteenth. Where are you going?"

"I'm not sure." Linda tilted her head. "I just needed to get away for a while. You know, escape from my life and just think. I'm headed for Montana, but eventually, I need to go back home to Philadelphia."

"I can relate."

"Why Alaska?" she asked

"It's a long story," I told her.

"Well," she said, glancing around, "it looks like we have some time. I'd love to hear it."

Suspicion flashed across my mind automatically. I had never told a complete stranger what had happened to me, not the whole truth. I'd explained briefly to the border guard and to the man at the campsite that I was traveling alone to get to Alaska, but never had anyone asked me why. I looked at Linda closely, counting on my intuition to guide me. She looked pure of heart and honest, and I felt safe. My mouth opened, and in the next period of time, out it all came.

"Me and my daughter are relocating after three men kidnapped us and held us hostage for a really long time." I paused to breathe and then I carried on. "They threatened to kill us and made me rob a bank. We needed to get away because we felt threatened and scared all the time, and I decided that taking us away from the pain back home was the best thing to do. My daughter is in Alaska with her grandmother. I took her there a week ago and went back home to move out of our house and get our stuff and then drive back to be with her. So here I am, escaping from my life, too." I'd spouted and gushed without looking up. Now I raised my eyes to hers.

"Oh, my God. You're not kidding, are you?" she said.

"I wish I was," I said.

"I can't believe you're out here on your own after something like that. That's awesome."

"Actually, " I said, "I never imagined doing this

myself, but this is bigger than me, bigger than anything. I know this is the plan for my life and I have to follow the whisper, the one that comes from a pure, loving place."

"It has to be right," she said, nodding.

"What about you? What's your story?"

"Well," said Linda, "I work in civil rights activism. Things have been so crazy. I just got back from Afghanistan and Columbia, documenting some stuff as a photojournalist. Then my relationship ended and I needed a break to figure things out. I guess we're kind of alike, you and me, 'cause I look to God and nature for my answers."

We were kindred spirits, that was clear. My long days of researching victims' laws at the local library while Breea was at school popped up in my mind as Linda talked about her journey as an activist. She'd been on the front lines, picketing for civil rights and taking a stand for what she believed was right. I knew I was headed in that direction, too, but when and how remained a mystery.

I was getting impatient waiting for the tow truck when a middle-aged couple walked up to us. The man had a rounded belly, a sign of a contented life, and he wore a friendly, fatherly grin. The woman, small and crisp looking, had woven one hand through his arm. The other held a leash with a small white dog at the end of it. She smiled and held up a coat hanger in the leash hand. "Need one of these?" she asked.

"How did you know?" I smiled broadly.

"We live across the river," said the man, "and we saw you out here. We figured you must be locked out of your car. It happens to people out here all the time."

The man slipped the coat hanger into the car door and fished it around. He wiggled it until it caught something, and then pulled. Voila! In seconds the lock popped up. I opened the door, and Haley jumped out, her tail wagging furiously. She bumped noses with the little white dog and took off like a shot for the water's edge, where she waded in up to her knees and drank greedily.

The tow truck pulled up, and I approached the driver, feeling a little guilty that we'd succeeded without him. I explained what had happened, apologized, and thanked him for coming. He shrugged, smiled wryly, and left. The older couple were already on their way back across the river and I called my thanks. They stopped on the bridge and waved. "Coffee tomorrow morning," called the woman, gesturing toward their house across the river. "Any time after dawn."

I turned to Linda. Without considering my manners, I invited her to join me at the campsite for supper with the people who had invited me. I didn't want her to leave because I had connected with her so strongly. That was unusual for me these days and I was willing to impose on my dinner invitation rather than see her drive off. I prayed that my hosts wouldn't mind. It just seemed like Linda and I still had a lot to talk about.

Dinner had cooled by the time we got back to the

campsite. My campmates greeted me with apologies for lukewarm food, and I apologized for being late.

"What happened?" the woman asked, seeming to be genuinely concerned. "We got worried about you."

I looked at her sheepishly. "You won't believe it," I said. "I locked myself out of my car, and this lady stopped to help me. This is Linda. Do you mind if she joins us?"

"Not at all," my host said, "but you'd better hurry unless you want it cold."

We sat down to chicken, sweet corn, and a delightful surprise, red wine. Linda and I devoured everything as we all talked and laughed about the adventures we were each having.

The couple had been traveling for weeks, something they did every summer. Linda described her life as an activist, and I rambled on about my daughter and my travels up the coast, but I steered clear of the actual reason I was living out of my car. We were a happy foursome until the couple went to bed soon after dinner. Then Linda and I took a walk around the campgrounds and eventually wound up back at my campsite.

"Mind if I crash here?" she asked, looking up at the darkening sky.

"Not at all. It's way too late to head out for Montana. Besides, we have a coffee date in the morning. Just grab your sleeping bag and put it in my tent."

"Great idea," said Linda. "You sure you're okay with that?"

"Absolutely."

Linda and I moved into my tent where we talked until dawn. I told her my story, she told me hers, and I felt that I'd met a fellow pilgrim along the treacherous road of life. For the first time in ages, I did not feel isolated and alone. I'll always remember Linda's last words before we drifted off to sleep. "Never give up fighting for what's right, Michelle."

It was the same kind of encouragement Breea had given me on that awful night. I was beginning to trust in the kindness of strangers again, grateful for the gentle reminder that there were wonderful people left in the world. Linda was one of them.

In the morning, we had a cup of coffee in the creekside home of the couple who had unlatched my door. When we said our good-byes, Linda was headed south, I was headed north, and we exchanged a long hug and our phone numbers. Although I'd met her less than twenty-four hours earlier, I knew I'd made a lifelong friend. To me, she represented a life well-lived, dedicated to fighting for what was right and true.

I drove away from the town of Hope, filled with the blessings of Linda and the others I'd met there. They would always be with me and I hoped that I would always be with them.

DURING the next few days, setting up my tent became second nature. I spent my days driving and when I'd settled into the local campsite in the evenings, I made friends with the families around me.

One family with three children made me miss Breea all the more, but I was getting closer to her by the moment.

"Cheese, crackers, and wine, Haley?" I asked my furry companion as I ate a cheap packaged snack and drank a miniature bottle of wine by my own tin-can campfire before sleep. I was celebrating having *fun*, a word I'd assumed was no longer in my vocabulary. I fell asleep listening to the crackling fire and the chirping of crickets, imagining Breea in my arms.

I drove on. The days went by and the distance between my little girl and me diminished. I photographed what appealed to me, and I made good time when the road was straight. One afternoon I came upon a small church with a white steeple and I stopped to take some pictures. Suddenly it started to rain and a young man on a bike rode up and stopped about fifty feet from my car. I'd passed him a little way back. His bike was packed like a miner's mule with a bedroll and camping gear. And did I mention that he was one of the best-looking men I'd seen in a long time?

"Hey," he called to me, "let's get to the café up the road before the storm hits. I'll buy you a cup of coffee."

I looked into his face to see if I could trust him.

"My name is Tom," he said.

"I'm Michelle. I can stay dry in my car, but I guess you're about to get drenched."

"Do you really want to drive into that?" He pointed

to a low, roiling gray sky. A dense grouping of heavy rain clouds darkened the horizon.

"Good point," I agreed. "I'll meet you there."

The storm clouds had opened and were dumping buckets of rainfall by the time we entered the café. A good piece of timing, I thought to myself. I probably wouldn't have pulled over if it hadn't been for Tom's invitation, and I'd be driving in a heavy downpour. Or I might have had to pull off the road somewhere to wait it out.

A heavyset woman wearing a white apron, with her dark hair pulled back in a ponytail, led us to a booth and took our order. Tom was on a three-month bicycling tour from Nova Scotia across Canada and Alaska, before heading back home to the eastern United States.

The rain was beating a rhythm on the roof of the café. Several more people rushed inside to escape the downpour, and in a few minutes, we found ourselves helping the only waitress pour coffee. We were having a great time, laughing and acting like we owned the place.

"This is kind of fun," I said to Tom as we passed each other holding coffeepots.

"Kinda? I'm having a blast! " He smiled ear-to-ear. I was stunned at how breathtakingly attractive he looked.

"More coffee, sir?" I kidded him.

"Why, certainly."

The woman with the ponytail came up to us. "You

two are great," she said. "I wish all my customers were so nice. Here's your soup. It's on the house."

When the rain finally stopped, Tom asked me to spend the rest of the day with him. I really wanted to say yes. He was gorgeous, he had treated me nicely, and he knew how to laugh and make the best of things. But I didn't *know* him. It wasn't safe, I decided. I declined his offer and said good-bye, explaining that I had to keep driving since my daughter's birthday was so close. I snapped his photo before I left and watched him mount his bike and begin to pedal.

My mind argued with my impulses for miles. I hadn't been in the company of a handsome man for an eternity, it seemed. I craved to be held and kissed and loved. "Go back and surprise him," an inner voice urged me. "You can't pass up an opportunity like this one. How often do they come around? It's just for one day, one night. Nothing has to happen. And if it does, so what? You'll never see him again."

My old self was kicking in, the one who got what she wanted with sexuality. It was the old me who attracted unhealthy relationships, found acceptance and love in ways that were defiling and always left me void. That part of me would find something good, destroy it quickly, and then run into the arms of some jerk who was completely bad for me. But I had decided to change all of that and I did not give in. This was my chance to start fresh, to make new choices, and to pay attention to a new code of honor. After all, I'd found out the hard way that "just one night" could

ruin my life. I shoved down my fantasies of what Tom
had in mind, how he looked naked, and everything
else about him. Rather, I cherished my newfound self-
respect and sense of safety. Nothing was worth losing
it again, but I had to admit, it sure felt good to look
across the table at a man once again, instead of cross-
ing the street to avoid him.

A few lakeside campsites later, canned lunches at
creekside picnic tables, and over hundreds of miles
across dirt, gravel, and potholes on the road known as
the Alcan (Alaska-Canada) Highway, I was within
hours of seeing my little girl. But I was nearly out of
gas and I'd all but used up the last of the money Kristi
had wired me. I hadn't anticipated the cost of gas in
Canada—triple what we paid in the states.

July 15, 2001
> *Breea's party starts at 3:00 PM and I promised to
> be there. With only twenty dollars left and three-
> quarters of a tank of gas, I may not make it. But I
> swear if I have to beg for the money, I'll be there for
> my daughter. I feel like I've let her down because we
> don't have a permanent home, but I'm going to
> change that as soon as I can.*

By noon I was completely broke. The little voice
that had gotten me on this road in the first place whispered, "Go to a church."

I laughed out loud. *Where am I going to find a
church*, I wondered.

I turned the corner and there stood a small white

stone community church. I blinked a few times to make sure I wasn't hallucinating. I'd heard about mirages in the desert and I wondered if I were imagining this because I wanted it so much. Then it dawned on me that it was Sunday. The parking lot was nearly full and I pulled into one of the few empty spots.

I walked to the front door of the church, grasped the handle on the heavy wooden church door, and opened it.

"Hello, young lady. What can I do for you?" A pastor greeted me.

I heard music coming from behind two doors leading to the main part of the church. I stumbled over my words a little until I got up my nerve. Then I inhaled and told the pastor why I was there.

"I've been on the road for days, and I need to get to my daughter in Anchorage by 3:00 PM for her birthday party. She turns eight today. She and I were attacked by masked gunmen and left our home to come to Alaska to heal and I've made it this far but I ran out of money and now I'm almost out of gas. So here I am."

He must have thought I was nuts, but he looked at me with a gentleness I can't describe. He touched my shoulder and said, "I'll be right back."

I stepped inside the church and sat in a pew next to an old man with twinkling eyes. I was singing with the congregation when the pastor tapped me on the shoulder and motioned for me to follow. I did, and he brought me to a man waiting in the foyer.

"This is Dave," said the pastor. "I think he can get you exactly what you need. God bless you, young lady, and good luck."

"Thank you so much." I was on the verge of tears.

"Follow me," said Dave. "Sounds like you need a full tank of gas, pretty lady."

I followed Dave to a nearby gas station where he filled my gas tank and paid for it. I cried with joy at his kindness, thanked him profusely, and drove for the next four hours without stopping.

Amid bears, glaciers, and rushing rapids that you usually only see in magazines, all I could see was Breea. I rolled up into the driveway honking my horn to let her know I was there, exhausted and exhilarated at the same time. Suddenly she was running toward me. Her laughter washed over me and her hugs reached into my heart as she ran out of the door, birthday hat on her head, arms outstretched. She was screaming, "Mommy! Mommy!" The citrus smell of her hair intoxicated me as I picked her up and swung her around, both of us sobbing with relief.

"I was afraid you wouldn't make it, Mommy," she said, swiping at the tears of joy running down my face. The family and a few of Breea's new friends from the neighborhood watched us, their own colorful party hats perched on their heads.

"We made a pinky promise," I reminded her.

"Mommy, I'm just opening my last present."

"No, you're not," I said. "Your last present is in the car."

After we tasted her Barbie birthday cake, I gave her the bright yellow fold-up scooter, and then we climbed in bed. Together we said our prayers, spoke our gratefulness, and sang "Somewhere over the Rainbow," our special version that I'd sung to her since the day she was born.

> *Somewhere over the rainbow*
> *Way up high,*
> *Mommy loves little Breea*
> *And sings her a lullaby.*

Then we shared one more birthday gift. With Breea's little legs wrapped around mine, we fell into dreamland in each other's arms, safe and sound.

10. Facing Demons

"CHRISTOPHER Butler has decided to represent himself in court. He has the right."

The voice on the other end of the line belonged to the DA, but it wasn't Joe Barends. He had unexpectedly retired and was no longer handling our case. This call from the new deputy district attorney handling our case, Tom Manning, came six months after I'd settled down with Breea in Alaska. This new maneuver by Butler, his decision to toy with the justice system, would cause the fourth postponement of our trial.

I rolled my eyes and fell into the nearest chair, understanding what that meant. The armed monster in the mask that put a gun to my head and proceeded to terrorize my child and me would be allowed to cross-examine me in the witness chair.

Tom's assurances that the criminal would be de-

My mom used to call us the seven little indians.
Photo courtesy of Linda Rae Foster

1994. On our own since Breea was a baby.
She is the love of my life.

October 2000. Breea in second grade, just before the crime.
This is the picture of her the prosecution used in court.

Just days before the attack in the house on Elevado Road.

1835 Elevado. Our house became a crime scene. Here you can see the back door where they broke in. The couch to the right is where we were sitting at the time of the break-in, our backs to the door. Behind the couch in the foreground, we stayed huddled all night at gunpoint, taped up and with a large dog circling us.
Photograph courtesy of San Diego District Attorney's Office.

These spears were used to intimidate us and meant to kill our dogs if they did not cooperate.
Photograph courtesy of San Diego District Attorney's Office.

The hoax dynamite sticks that were taped to our bodies.
Photograph courtesy of San Diego District Attorney's Office.

The closet. This is where
Breea was placed when
I was forced to leave
the house and rob the bank.
She was still in the closet
when I returned.
*Photograph courtesy of San Diego
District Attorney's Office.*

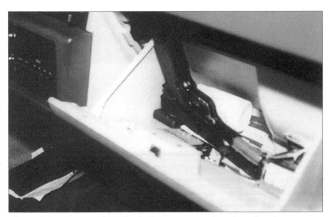

One of the guns used in the kidnapping was found in the glove compartment of Butler's car when he was pulled over and arrested along with Lisa Ramirez, who was later acquitted.

Photograph courtesy of San Diego District Attorney's Office.

A search revealed a mountain of physical evidence.

Photograph courtesy of San Diego District Attorney's Office.

First Christmas after the crime, in the hotel in Carlsbad.
My eyes say it all. I was devastated.

Two weeks after arriving in Alaska.
Notice the color of my hair and how short Breea's hair is.

When the papers printed a photo of Butler on the stand, I scribbled over his suit and tie and wrote, "I wish the jury could see him the way he looked the night he attacked us!"

The prosecution team celebrated victory. It was a bittersweet time for me. From left to right: Tom Manning, Rudy Zamora, courtroom bailiff, Me, Diane Jimenez, case detective, FBI Special Agent Jeff Higgins.
Photograph courtesy of San Diego District Attorney's Office.

Taking time out for what matters most as we leave
Mom's hometown in Maine.

March 2006. The two of us, focused on a positive future.

fending himself in shackles and handcuffs did not make me feel any better. I could not get over the fact that at this stage in the game Christopher Butler was being granted the right to play attorney. That meant he could victimize me all over again in the courtroom with the judge and jury looking on. It sounded like a three-ring circus and I was the main event, a wild animal being whipped and beaten into submission.

"You're kidding me, right?" I said.

"I wish I was," said Tom Manning.

"*Un*fucking believable!" I hung up the receiver with a disgusted, frustrated thud.

WHEN I arrived in Alaska we were told we had three months until the criminal trial started back in San Diego. I was naive about judiciary protocol and believed we would be back home by September. That meant we had the summer to explore the Alaskan frontier and reconnect with the nature that I had loved as a child. Breea and I took advantage of every moment, not knowing it would be a full year before the justice system could get things in order. Breea had to start school in Alaska and the small mountain-based elementary school was perfect for her. So was her teacher, Ms. Reizer.

"We are new to Alaska," I told her in a private meeting, "and Breea and I are recent violent crime victims. She needs a little more nurturing than usual and she has trouble using the bathroom by herself."

Ms. Reizer smiled reassuringly at me. "Come in tomorrow morning with Breea at seven forty-five," she said. "Everything will be fine."

The next morning we sat with Breea's new teacher at a small round table inside the classroom. "Hi Breea," she said. "Your mom told me some stuff that happened to you back in San Diego. Would you like to talk about it a little?"

"Well," she said, looking first at me and then at Ms. Reizer, "three guys came in our house and taped us up and scared me so bad."

"And now you are here and safe, right?" asked the teacher.

"Right," Breea said in a lively tone.

Ms. Reizer spoke slowly and calmly. "What I want you to know," she said, "is that you don't have to be embarrassed about what happened to you. It's okay to ask if a buddy can go with you to the bathroom, or to tell me when you feel sick because you're remembering things that happened. It's always okay for you to talk to me. I'm a safe person for you to come to for help. By the way, lots of the kids are brand new because their parents are in the military and they move a lot. They're a little nervous too, just like you. I bet you will make friends fast, though, because you're nice and funny and smart. Okay, sweetie?"

"Okay," Breea said easily. She looked relaxed.

Ms. Reizer was young, a first-time teacher, and she knew Breea would struggle in a different way than most kids. That was true, but time, and places like Alaska, can heal invisible wounds in the most fascinating way. Breea quickly found comfort at her new school and she told stories about her new friends, seemingly forgetting all about life back in California.

Finally at ease with Breea's situation, I used every ounce of my strength to focus on being in Alaska, not San Diego. I decided to pursue a lifelong dream, to get my general equivalency diploma (GED). One of my life's greatest disappointments was not graduating. I wanted to look better on paper when I applied for my next job, whatever it would be.

I'd believed that I was living up to my potential in my life, in my career as a banker, that I was intelligent, and that my future was filled with countless possibilities. I could hide under my business suit and no one would ever guess by looking at me that my past was tainted with shame, ugliness, pain, and the fact that I was a high school dropout. I'd climbed up the ladder of corporate America using my intellect and instincts. But each time I'd had to fill out an application for work, I was aware of my lack of higher education.

Not that I'd had much of a choice. I knew that leaving school for a full-time job and escaping from my dad and my abusive first boyfriend was exactly what I'd needed to do back then. I'd wanted to graduate but I just couldn't. Now I had a chance. I decided to be fully qualified in the future, since returning to the banking industry was out of the question. And so, at age thirty-five, just like my daughter, I was a student again.

I passed all my tests with flying colors. I had to

laugh that although I'd had success in the world of numbers, my scores in math were the lowest of all. It was a good thing that my banking job was more about customer service and less about number crunching or I'd never have made it past bank teller school. Now, after some focused studying and passing all my tests, I got to put on the blue cap and gown and have my picture taken with my diploma in hand.

I was thrilled when I applied to Alaska University and was accepted. Now I had to figure out what to major in and my mother-in-law was the perfect person on which to bounce off some ideas.

"Try something you love honey," she counseled. "You like to take pictures and write. You're outgoing and I think working with people would be great for you."

I thought a moment about what I really loved to do. "Photography would work," I agreed, "but it's so competitive and I'm already in my thirties. I love to write and I like public speaking. Maybe politics or law . . ."

"Sweetie," Judy interrupted me, "the trial isn't even here yet. You don't know what it will be like and how it will affect you."

"You're right," I said. "Those jobs still hit too close to home for me. Maybe marketing or advertising, something I've already done in banking that can carry over."

"That sounds perfect for you," Judy said.

This tiny woman who stood five feet tall and weighed about a hundred pounds soaking wet was the kindest, sweetest person I ever knew. She generally sounded like the voice of reason to me and we stayed close despite the divorce and the death of Breea's grandpa. With Judy and Breea cheering me on, I made a decision. I signed up for my major in communications with an emphasis on public relations.

The first day I walked into the classroom, the stadium seating I'd seen only on television overwhelmed me. I was in COLLEGE, one of only a few students in our thirties, surrounded by a bunch of younger kids who had no idea why they were there. Although I knew that youth was a challenge in itself, I have to admit I felt somewhat resentful of the annoying drivel of my younger fellow students.

I made fast friends with my professor, however, a wonderful, intelligent quick-witted woman who became one of my greatest cheerleaders. I was so enthralled with my critical writing class and learning all about American media that sometimes I forgot about the shadow of the looming trial. It was comforting being in the wide-open spaces of the last frontier, with regular phone sessions with my therapist back in San Diego. I had a newfound excitement about my place on the campus scene and I was beginning to blossom into someone I had never known—Michelle Renee.

July 30, 2001

Since arriving back in Alaska, I've seen a bald eagle soaring, a giant moose feeding at the side of the road and a red fox scurrying by with freshly caught prey hanging from his mouth. Snow white

mountain goats gracefully climb impossibly vertical
rocks and icebergs shimmer blue in the ocean while
the glaciers are too vast and numerous to name. I
have heard rushing waters with salmon fighting
their way upstream with strength and determination.
The most impressive sight of all is Breea's smile and
the way she sleeps through the night, untroubled.

We took full advantage of our time to explore the vast Alaskan wilderness. Sitting at a small roadside café after lunch one day, I asked Breea, "Want to go on an adventure?"

"Sure Mommy," she said. "Where?"

"Well, I'm not sure honey. Let's head north and see where we end up."

"That sounds fun. Just you and me, Mommy?"

"Yup, just you and me."

We drove to Mt. McKinley and stayed in a rustic cabin, reminiscent of the cabins of the Alaskan gold rush era. There was no water, no lights, nothing, and we had a blast. We shopped, we ate, and we climbed as high as we could. We stood on what felt like the top of the world, taking it all in together, just like we used to. As autumn turned into winter, the snowfall settled upon us, a thick white blanket covering the earth, disguising the ice underneath. We hiked up glaciers and explored ice caves. We strolled along paths that led to incredible waterfalls.

When winter arrived, the brutal cold and unrelenting darkness of the long Alaskan winter felt safe and cozy. I focused on the beauty of undisturbed nature and my newfound freedom from fear. I'd take the cold with its sparkling snows and clear view of the Northern Lights any day, if Breea and I could continue to fall asleep at night with peace in our hearts.

Thanksgiving was approaching when I got a surprise letter from my mom. She wanted to come for a visit, but I was reluctant. My mom had been distant during the entire kidnapping ordeal and its aftermath and I didn't know why. Breea and I were still fragile, and there was no telling what effect Alaska would have on my mother. It was a place she'd visited as a child with her father, and who knew what memories would be triggered if she came to visit?

Ultimately, I agreed to let Mom come and be with us. I was glad I did, because from the moment she arrived, it was obvious she needed a rest, just as I had. I made her comfortable. She was on the top of a list I had compiled of "people I needed to forgive and ask for their forgiveness." I felt this was crucial to my commitment to have healthier relationships and better boundaries.

After Mom slept off her journey, we reminisced and laughed together. She talked to me openly and honestly about her past for the first time, ever. We cried copious tears of regret, love, and grief. Finally, I could understand as she filled me in on things I never knew about her. I was rapt with her stories, able to appreciate another side of her.

"I will never have another love like Bill," my mom said of her forbidden relationship with the father of my oldest sister, a married man twice her age. "I wasn't ashamed about the affair or having his baby. Everyone else had a problem with it and then your dad came along at the right time, I guess. He was handsome and said all the right things. But by the time I realized he was battling some powerful demons and blind rages, I was trapped. It was too late. I never really recovered from his abuse."

It was a whole new experience for my mom to confront her past, and we became closer as we found common ground. I, too, had been involved in an affair with a married man for several years, a fact that I shared with her for the first time. But there was so much more to talk about, so many questions about my childhood.

"Mom, remember when I saw you coming down the hall in the morning when we lived on Big Rock Road and you were all bloody."

"Yes," she said, looking away. My mom was tough as nails. Crying had never come easily to her and this time was no different. "That morning," she said with dry eyes, "has haunted me for years. I had another confrontation with your dad. He said I deserved it for rejecting him. I always wondered how that moment affected you. I remember your eyes and the way you looked at me and I wondered if you even remembered. I was too ashamed to talk about it until now."

My throat closed up and I couldn't speak. I wanted to hug her, but I couldn't remember how, since we hadn't done much touching for years. The whole family had become numb and now, that *had* to change.

"How did you do it?" I finally asked her. "For all those years, Mom. All the violence and seeing your kids being beat down. Do you know how scared I was when you had to walk to work in the middle of the night. I saw your bloody heels and the broken blisters. I wanted to make it all better for you somehow, Mom. I wanted to take care of you."

My mother heaved a huge sigh. "Honestly," she said, "I have no idea what kept me going except my kids. I tell you, there were times I didn't want to live anymore. But you know that already. I was miserable for a very long time, even after both suicide attempts failed. But I'm still alive for a reason. I'm finally drug-free and I'm trying to figure it all out, just like you are. Hell, at least you are not sixty and only just getting to it, like I am. You got me beat on that one."

We chuckled.

I quickly said, "I want you to read something I wrote. It's called *When Knives Talk*. I too was suicidal after the crime, and I just wanted it all to stop, to have one single moment of mental peace. But suicide wasn't the answer. I could never do that to Breea. I know now that ending my life is not about peace. Real peace is in here." I pointed to my heart. I handed her a poem I'd written called *Mommy Please*, in which I described how much I wanted to be happy again, how I wanted her to stop going back to him, and how much my own daughter wanted to know her.

I knew my words had touched her deeply, when she looked up at me with tears in her eyes. We opened our arms and held on to one another. "Can we forgive and never look back?" I asked.

"That is exactly what we can do."

"Let's go for a walk," I suggested.

I watched her from several steps behind as we trudged through the snow together. Her hands were buried in the pockets of her thick coat, and her breath came in thin white puffs, wafting past her head and vanishing. We walked along the soft white earth, in silence. It was a very good day.

M Y mom could not stay through Christmas but she helped us decorate the tree. Each time an ornament went up, more of her defenses went down. It was as if she were melting like a snowman in the sun, and I wished she could stay until there was nothing left of her icy past. In the most magical setting, I caught glimpses of the soft woman buried deep down inside of her when she wasn't panicked or obsessed with survival. There was the woman who had sung and danced with me in the living room of my childhood, filled with hopes and dreams. Oh, how I had missed her! And best of all, her relationship with Breea had begun to flower as we got ready for a very white Christmas in Alaska.

On our way to the airport the day Mom was leaving, she talked lovingly about her hometown in New England. I strengthened my resolve to bring her back home one day to face her own twisted past. When we'd been there last, just Breea and me, we'd visited

Mom's high school and looked through the yearbook archives to find her class picture. I'd phoned some of her old friends and met with them, gathering as much information about my mother as I could. I'd even gone to the old house where she'd grown up and the current owner had been happy to guide me through. This was where she ran and played, I thought to myself, back when she was no older than Breea.

When I waved good-bye to my mother, my anger toward her was gone, and so was hers toward me. As much as I wished she would stay longer, I comforted myself by seeing that the woman who took off for California was in much better shape than when she'd arrived. I knew that as soon as I could, I'd take her to Maine for the first time in forty-three years, to her hometown, to the place in which she could rediscover her roots. Most of all, she needed to ask the man she loved most to forgive her—her father.

I can't imagine we will ever again enjoy Christmas as much as we did that winter in Alaska. The previous year had been filled with terror, but now we were far, far away from the ghosts that had haunted us. Time, distance, and loving family were calming our shattered nerves and soothing our shattered souls.

Breea ice-skated on the streets on Christmas Eve and Christmas Day with other people brave enough to weather the bone-chilling cold. We sledded down the hills and had fierce snowball fights. It all seemed so Norman Rockwell—perfect.

When Dave called, he spoke in a weary tone, wishing us a happy holiday. I could tell he needed help, my help, so I offered him the last of my frequent-flier miles to get on a plane and visit us. Of all the people in my life back home, I missed him (and Kristi) the most and I wanted him with us. This place seemed to have inexplicable healing powers and new beginnings were something of a theme that season.

As I drove to the airport to pick Dave up, I was aware of how rarely we saw each other when we'd lived a couple of hours apart. We barely knew each other before the crime and now it had brought us together. Besides, Alaska attracted the weary like a magnet, drawing people who needed to mend, which seemed to be the better part of my nuclear family.

"Hey, buddy. How's it going?" I asked him as we picked up his luggage at baggage claim. I thought he looked broken, and I knew he'd been struggling with a bad relationship for four years. I also knew that his spiritual life was practically nonexistent and he was plagued with drug addiction like others in the family. I learned soon after he landed that his employer had just laid him off and he'd been severely depressed in recent weeks. He needed a break and we needed each other. I could relate to his struggle with darkness and drugs but he didn't know that yet.

"You look great, Mi," he said, using my nickname. "Wow, your hair is turning blonde again."

I nodded my head and said, "I'm starting to be someone I recognize." We both knew I was talking about more than my hair color. Dave's trademark bear hug engulfed me, and I smelled his cologne that reminded me of the best parts of home.

"Come here you little cutie," Dave said as he swung Breea around.

"I love how you smell Uncle Dave." Breea said it for me. "And I missed you so much."

His attitude right then, in the midst of his own depression, was the essence of Dave. He was consistently nice, a guy whom everyone liked and good-looking enough to catch the eye of my girlfriends when we were growing up. A rugged, outdoorsy man who had always loved fishing and hunting, he would revel in Alaska once his troubles lifted enough for him to open his eyes and look around.

"You okay?" I asked.

"I'm beat down, Michelle," he admitted. "Thanks so much for getting me up here. If you only knew where I was a couple of weeks ago. But that doesn't matter now because here I am. It was a long flight, so let's go check this place out." With pools of joy welling up in his eyes, he said, "It's so good to see you."

"You, too, Dave," I echoed. "You, too."

We talked in the car all the way to Judy's house. He was happy for me that I was doing better and I saw how proud he was when I showed him my diploma. Beyond that, however, he was quiet and he kept to himself at first. I eventually managed to get him out hiking, dancing, and listening to lively music at one of my favorite new hideaway spots where you could get the best fresh fish in town. And he seemed absolutely jovial when he and Breea built a great big snowman with a real corncob pipe.

"Why couldn't we have grown up this way?" he said to me when I came out to see their handiwork. Together, we watched Breea pack more snow on the finished snowman, prolonging her enjoyment, unwilling for the project to be over.

"We needed activities but we never had any," said Dave. "Why couldn't they have played with us and taught us to laugh?"

Why indeed?

I could see that Dave was getting ready to let his guard down, just like my mother had done a few weeks earlier. Within days, the sparkle had returned to his eyes and his cheeks were a healthy color of pink. In the evenings, we talked late into the night and he began to share with me some of his challenges and personal disappointments. He spoke about how he felt my mom had shunned him since his early childhood because he was David *Jr.* He revealed his lifelong struggle to gain her approval and how much these problems had wounded him and ruined his relationships with women.

I was stunned when he told me with a quivering chin how much the break-in and the way I'd handled it had affected him. He had seen my life up close for the first time in our adult life and apparently, I had inspired him to change. "I've never seen anything like it Michelle," he said. "Your faith, your courage, and what an amazing mom you've been through it all. You are such a gift to my life and I just want you to know that."

Now I had something for him. "Do you have any idea that you're my hero?" I asked. "You were the only one who came to my rescue when I needed someone the most. I'm so proud to have you as my brother."

"Do you remember when you grabbed that napkin and began to obsessively sketch a picture of you and Breea holding on to one another that day in your dining room at the beach house?"

"Yeah," I replied, remembering how I used those obsessive impulses to get the images out of my head.

"Well," he said, "I never told you this but I heard an inner message when you were drawing that said, '*Look, she draws for me now.*'"

I was amazed. He was hearing an inner voice too.

Finally, we got to the nitty gritty when I told him my earlier painful and terrifying suicidal tendencies. He broke down and told me that two weeks ago he was on the floor of his garage with a gun in his mouth, ready to pull the trigger. But when I instinctively invited him to Alaska and gave him a free ticket, he symbolically had stepped away from the ledge.

If anyone understood the pull of "the ledge," it was me. I had been there, particularly on Easter weekend, on a trip with Kristi and her family. I could see myself, bloody, lying on the kitchen floor while everyone else was jovial, enjoying life. I called for help that night and could see the pain in Dave's eyes. I knew that look and flashed back to my mom with her bloated body, dripping charcoal on a gurney. We had to be strong for each other. Like me, he was the single parent of a child, a son that he adored more than anything in his life. But trying to make it all work with an obvious void of life-managing tools was sometimes more than we could bear. I recalled that earlier that year, I'd had a sense that one day, Dave and I were destined to work together. I'd told him as much, but now I knew in what capacity we would do so. It actually had come to me back home in San Diego one Sunday morning a few months after the crime. It was an organization I was determined to develop to provide victims of violent crimes with what they really needed—the physical, emotional, and spiritual support that I didn't get.

I'd gone over my original "if-only" list.

If only someone had been there for Breea and me to make sure we had timely trauma counseling, a safe place to live, and a home for Charlie, our dog.

If only we'd been told to take self-defense classes to bolster our self-confidence.

If only someone had arranged food deliveries and babysitting services when we were too traumatized to do it ourselves.

If only someone had been there to assure us that our seemingly over-the-top reactions to noises and strangers were normal after such an event!

Not only did we get none of those things, we remained in physical danger until the gang members who had so traumatized us were apprehended. Not an ounce of help or protection was offered or proffered, which sounded like a crime in itself.

Since coming to Alaska with nothing but time on my hands, I'd decided to step up my research efforts. On the days I had no classes, I'd drop Breea at school and then spend the rest of the day in Judy's computer room, reading and studying. The statistics of work-related violent crimes were staggering—as high as 18 percent. According to the FBI, banks were targeted every twenty minutes in the United States, and by 2003, robberies and other violent crimes had increased 7.2 percent nationwide.

I ascertained pretty quickly that there was no system in place for psychological trauma or injuries of the sort that I had suffered, and there was no employer accountability whatsoever. I read warnings that had been distributed in 1997 by the FBI and the FDIC (Federal Deposit Insurance Corporation) alerting the entire banking industry about the type of crime of which I'd been a victim. In fact, there was crime story after crime story on television and in newspapers of people being brutalized and having their lives ripped to shreds, and not only by criminals. They were also let down by a system that was supposed to protect them.

A familiar anger resurfaced. I wanted to make a difference as I fantasized pounding my fists on wooden podiums and demanding changes. The words "protecting liquid assets" that were all over the outdated Bank Protection Act of 1968 fueled my ambition. What good would liquid assets do if a person were too traumatized and wounded emotionally to live a functional life?

I also raged at the fact that until I met Iby in the hallway of the trauma center, no one had mentioned word one to me about post-traumatic stress disorder. I'd learned that it affected nearly every crime victim, thousands of people a day, and no one was talking about it. That was about to change, right after I absorbed a load of technical information that would help me shed light on what was missing in the banking industry, one that was so intensely crime-targeted. I wanted help not only for my daughter and me, but I felt I owed it to all victims to be their voice in a society that shuns victims, leaving them to languish unprotected in the shadows of pro-prisoner laws and rights. Victims needed someone with a voice and I was determined to sing.

Each day, I made my way through enormous stacks of paperwork to establish a nonprofit corporation. I organized my vision on a fifteen-page website that I taught myself to build through trial and error. Then, after filing for a 501(c)(3) tax exempt organization status, I could accept donations, even online. I was on my way. I was also in over my head, but I used the resources I could find—friends, attorneys, clerks—and before I knew it, the foundation was approved and ready to roll. And so was Dave.

"Hey, I want to show you something," I said one morning after I'd taken Breea to school. I brought him into the computer room and unveiled the stacks of paperwork I was compiling.

He was amazed. "See what I mean, Mi," he said. "I've never seen anything like it. You are a dynamo."

"Actually," I corrected him, "it's a God thing. And as long as you don't say I have a *dynamite* personality, we're okay."

We both laughed. It felt nice to be gaining back a healthy sense of humor, especially about the crime.

"What can I do to help?" he asked sincerely. And at that, the door to our partnership opened wide.

For the last several days of his stay in Alaska, Dave and I holed up in a twelve-by-twelve room, assembling binders, designing a logo, and printing brochures and business cards. When we took breaks in between our long creative brainstorming sessions, I caught a glimpse of the real Dave, playing with Breea, dancing in the snow, gazing out across the vast, brilliant glaciers and watching Alaskan eagles soar.

"Where do you think we will be a year from now?" he asked with soft, caring eyes.

"I'm not sure, Dave. It really isn't up to us is it?"

"No, it's not."

We looked out at what was in front of us, knowing that when we got back home, people would try to discourage our efforts. We knew that what we were setting up would involve battling at the highest political levels, but I didn't care and neither did he. We had a mission and nothing could stop us.

When we saw Dave off at the airport, he promised to continue supporting our vision. We both understood our uphill battle. The recent 40 percent national budget cuts to most community crime victim organizations were partly to blame. State and local government agencies were so backed up with crime victims there was no hope for a speedy review, yet another issue I vowed to tackle when my foundation was up and running. With all of my years working in the financial industry, I could use my experience to help others avoid my fate by pushing for new laws.

As I watched Dave heading toward security before he got on the plane, I noticed how different he looked from when he had arrived. His shoulders were back, his head was held high, and he looked refreshed, relaxed, and fit for battle. A fire of purpose burned inside him. It felt like something was shaking my family tree, as the old leaves fell and new ones budded, right before my eyes.

I drove back to Judy's home feeling as if my life were starting to make sense. I passed the snow-covered trees as the landscape stretched out before me like a great big Eskimo Pie. Healing had happened for my family and me in this brave, wild new world. My mom and I had delicately opened a box of secrets, settled our lifelong conflict. Breea was sleeping through the nights and laughing through the days. Dave was smiling again, drug free, and working with me to make a difference in the world. The voice inside with which I had previously lost contact was back, to support me and, once again, to become my guide.

Three months later, Breea and I took to the sky headed for San Diego, our tickets paid for by the prosecution.

11. Opening Arguments

THE defense was up to no good. They so manipulated the law for the sake of freeing scum; I was beginning to understand why victims often dropped criminal charges before their cases ever made it to trial. Some never even filed charges because of the cruelty toward victims in the courtroom. Bottom line: a victim's search for closure could not be found in our justice system as it existed. Why do you think so many people call it the "criminal" justice system instead of the "American" justice system?

My case was no exception, but there was no way I was not going forward. Along with my personal list of reasons, I had to set an example for Breea. She needed to see that I would follow through and seek justice for the wrong that was done to her and her mother. But each time we thought we might finally start the trial, a phone call would come postponing it.

Late in the afternoon of August 24, 2001, a month before the trial date was set for the fourth time, I was still in Alaska. I'd chaperoned a field trip for Breea's class and we were both in a great mood when we pulled into Judy's driveway. When I turned off the engine, I heard the phone ringing so I rushed into the house and caught it on the fourth ring. "Hello?" I said breathlessly, still invigorated by being in the Alaskan wilderness.

I caught my breath when I heard Tom Manning's voice. He was a nice enough man, but he sounded less than enthusiastic. "The trial is postponed, again." he said. "The judge tentatively reset it for January, 7, 2002."

My heart sank. The crime had happened fourteen months ago. Where was the swift justice, the speedy trial that American jurisprudence promised? Would we spend the rest of our lives waiting for this awful event? It seemed that I had no choice but to live my life around each new date.

The good news, if you could call it that, was that Butler had had a change of heart. When he realized the large amount of tangible, physical evidence the DA's office had gathered against him, he knew he needed a real attorney. The trial was postponed while he got himself another public defender. The other three also had decided to switch public defenders one more time, causing more delays.

When the real date rolled around, after having spent the last several weeks preparing my testimony, we flew back to San Diego. We spoke of our excitement to be heading back to our hometown mixed with apprehension about being back in the place where the worst thing in our life occurred, and went straight from the airport to a hotel. The painful patterns reemerged as we entered the vicinity where the crime had happened, but we were no longer in shock and impossible terror. I was distraught when we both began sleeping badly and Breea clung to me in the night more tightly than she had in months. But even when my sensitivity to strange noises came back, I knew we were in the home stretch, headed for closure. We had to face our demons and make sure these monsters stayed behind bars for as long as possible.

Breea swam in the pool with her cousin Shawn, Dave's son, while I spent my days pouring over documents the prosecutors wanted me to review to jog my memory. As if my memory needed any more jogging! But I read and read so I would be prepared. Little did I know that a lifetime of preparation would not have been enough, but Dave was right there, offering to help in any way he could. He even suggested that he move in with us while the trial was on and I gladly took him up on his offer. If there was one thing I'd learned in all of this, it was to ask for and accept help. I really needed Dave, and the closer the trial got, the more troubling the flashbacks and nightmares became.

I knew my work was cut out for me but I was bent

on staying positive. With the overflowing evidence the prosecutors had in their possession as well as signed confessions from three out of the four accused, it was realistic to expect that we could put these people away for life. That was why I turned down all plea bargain deals from the defense attorneys. I received a phone call one afternoon from the deputy district attorney while Breea, Kristi, and I were shopping at the mall, trying to distract ourselves. He asked if I would accept a plea bargain from Lisa, the woman involved, who had agreed to testify against the others, including her own boyfriend.

I was stunned at what he was suggesting—that I should agree to a twelve-year sentence for this woman who had plotted with the rest of them. On good behavior, she could get out in six years. Where would we be in six years? Still dealing with the trauma, while she was walking free? This woman had been outside all the time, in a car, while she knew what was happening to us. She had not only allowed it, she had *enabled* it. Twelve years wasn't nearly enough time for her.

"But Michelle," he argued with me, "if we give Lisa a reduced sentence, she'll still be spending a chunk of time in prison. Why not accept the plea bargain and use her as a snitch?"

I thought about it for a whole thirty seconds. The answer was NO. I wanted them off the streets forever, including her. With so much incriminating evidence, I was sure, along with the rest of the prosecution team, that she would be found guilty on all counts. But I *didn't* know her confession would never be seen by the jury. In fact, the charges against her had nothing to do with conspiracy. It was as if she had been in the house, too, since there were no accessory charges either, but this would have been impossible to prove or convict on. To deem our prosecution system as flawed was a pathetic understatement.

I stuck to my guns. No plea bargains. I reminded him that plea bargains were out of the question, especially since he himself had agreed there was enough physical evidence to make the conviction a "slam dunk." I wondered who in the world Lisa would have to snitch on, anyway, since everyone was already identified and the court held three signed confessions. Most importantly, why should *she* get a break when Breea and I didn't get one? I had no interest in making her life easier since she'd been partially responsible for making mine unbearable. They all deserved to languish behind bars for a good long time, Lisa included, and I was prepared to take it all the way.

In hindsight, I can see that my greatest strength was my determination. But my greatest weakness was my ignorance about what defense attorneys were capable of and allowed to do.

OPENING arguments began on Monday, June 3, 2002, thirty-one months after the crime. The principals gathered at the courthouse and I had to go there to identify the accused, two of them by height and build, since they were wearing masks and I never saw their faces. Butler and Ramirez, however, I could identify by sight since they had been in the bank to see me.

I clutched a picture of Breea that she'd stuck in my hand when I was escorted out of our hotel room. A detective from the prosecution task force led me into an unmarked vehicle that would take me to court and bring me back. I'd managed to swallow some oatmeal before I left, but it did nothing for my light-headedness or my perpetually upset stomach. When I saw the large white courthouse looking ahead, I could almost feel the buzz of activity by the robed judges, uniformed bailiffs, and fast-talking attorneys as they prepared for what I perceived as a bunch of bad guys.

I held Breea's photo tighter when I became aware that trucks were pulling up in the back, letting out prisoners in orange jumpsuits and chains. This would be the first time I'd be near my tormentors since that night. How would I react? Would their family members be there to support them? Would their gang buddies try to intimidate me? I felt apprehensive about all of it, but worse about the fact that for the first time since the attack, I would see their faces without masks.

True, I'd seen their pictures in the paper and I'd talked to Christopher Butler and Lisa Ramirez in the bank before the break-in, but that was a long time ago, a year and seven months to be exact. Nearly six hundred days had passed since these felons had invaded my life and changed it forever.

I stared out of the car window, shaking, and settled

my focus on my shoes. I needed to get the heel on my left shoe fixed. *Maybe I'm not ready for this.* It didn't matter. This was it. I got out of the car. The door slamming made me jump. I tried to regulate my breath as I stepped into the elevator. It was hard to breathe, as if I were in a bad dream, gasping for air, the same feeling I had when we were kidnapped. I couldn't escape then and I couldn't escape now. I was led to a wooden door at the end of a long corridor. The gold engraved sign read Courtroom 17. My escort, a member of the prosecution team, gestured with a swoop of his left arm and I entered.

The room smelled like paper and leather, overlain with a faint mixture of cologne, aftershave, and carpet cleaner. I stared down at the burnished wood of the barrier that separated the onlookers from the rest of the courtroom as I passed through the squeaky swinging gate. This was the last phase of an excruciatingly drawn-out process. In this room, the fate of our tormentors would be decided. I did not want to look up. What if they were already there, standing a few feet away?

To my right, there were empty chairs where the defendants would sit. I exhaled. They weren't in the room yet, but the public defenders were. They must have had no consciences at all to defend such terrible people. I tried to focus on the dozen strangers in the elevated seats at the left side of the room: the jury. They stared back at me, sizing me up like I was an object. The gentle face and grin of the bailiff eased my tension slightly as he led me to my designated spot in the room, straight across from the men and a woman who had plotted for months to destroy us.

Nearby was the sharply dressed Tom Manning, the prosecuting deputy district attorney. When I extended my hand to him, his gaze was gentle, kind. That helped. He moved in an easy, agile manner, consummately self-assured. Just behind him were Detective Rudy Zamora, FBI Agent Jeff Higgins, and Diane, Tom's assistant. They smiled at me in a way that told me, *"You can do this. Go get 'em Michelle."* I didn't want to disappoint them. We'd been through a lot together.

We waited for the judge but my attention was riveted to a door with a small wired-glass panel. At long last, the defendants were led in and seated, with Butler's chains clanking. He had tried to escape, so they would not unchain him. I did not look into his eyes, but because they haunted me so much, I could see them anyway.

"All rise, " the bailiff ordered. We stood in deference to the female judge who was entering the courtroom. She looked stern. I resisted a powerful urge to bolt headlong from the courtroom, snapping my attention to the industrial-looking clock on the wall. I took a deep breath. In a couple of weeks, I told myself, this will be over and I can walk around free as a bird, while these men and that misguided woman who helped them would be sleeping on prison cots and eating brown and white food for years to come. That kind of pep talk was how I kept myself calm enough to stay in the room.

I breathed deeply, reminding myself that very soon, I'd be leaving the courtroom anyway, since I would not be testifying for three more days. I was labeled the "key witness for the State of California." That meant that I would make this one appearance in the courtroom to identify the perpetrators and would not be allowed back until I took the stand.

Tom gently took my arm and turned me in the direction of where the defendants were now standing in a line-up. I lifted my head and looked, really looked, at the three men. I nearly smiled when I wondered, how did *they* like being held against *their* will? They sure as hell weren't grunting out orders now like they had on that tortuous night.

Christopher Huggins, aka Big Hershey, was a massively large man with no trace of emotion on his face.

Robert Arthur Ortiz, gang moniker Bones, was wearing professor-type spectacles, his thick dark braids pulled back from his face with a rubber band. If it were possible, he looked even skinnier than I remembered, almost insubstantial.

And there was Christopher Butler, the "talker," and leader of the pack, a badly disturbed man with ugly eyes, who for some reason appeared to want to destroy me. What did I mean to him? When I looked directly at him, I instinctively stepped backward, my flight response triggered by the anger in his face and the memory of trauma that was deeply etched into my brain. I got control of myself. I had a job to do. I needed to identify these male defendants who entered our house so we could go forward with the trial. *God I wish everyone could see the way they looked that night,* I thought to myself, *like pathetic, degenerative monsters.* It took every ounce of my strength and will just to stand still.

"Ms. Renee, raise your right hand please," the bailiff said.

I did.

"Do you swear to tell the truth, the whole truth, and nothing but the truth so help you God?"

"I do, so help me God . . ." *So help me God.* It echoed across the room and in my mind. I turned to Tom. My throat was closing up and I was trembling uncontrollably. "What do you want me to do?" I whispered.

"Are these men approximately the same height and weight as the three men who violently burst through the back door of your home on November 21, 2000?" he asked me in a strong professional voice.

I nodded and said yes. Then I covered my mouth with my hand, swallowing the bile that had risen up into my throat.

"In your opinion," he continued, "are these the men responsible for what happened during that night of terror and what took place the following morning?"

"Yes."

Tom touched my arm and said softly, "It's okay, Ms. Renee. Thank you. You can go now."

Without another glance toward the prisoners, I turned my back and was led to the witness room. Breea's picture was now a crunched ball of paper in my sweaty hands. I opened up the tight ball, trying to draw strength from the image of her face. I wanted so much to take her pain away, to erase what they had done to her. But that little seven-year-old girl was gone. In her place was a child who knew the world could be vicious, a little girl with only me to count on—and I wasn't about to let her down. I touched the picture softly with my finger.

I sat in the cold, stark white witness room for a while, pondering the fact that it had been almost a year to the day that we had escaped with a new identity, and almost two years since the kidnapping. I wiped the tears that were streaming down my face, dripping onto the smooth surface of the table beneath my elbows. I tilted my head back and tried to regain my composure while I waited to be driven back to the hotel. I could hear the words *I believe in you* replaying in my mind. It was Dave's reassuring voice. As usual, he was keeping his promise, and he would be there every step of the way, from the beginning of our hell to the last sound of the gavel in Courtroom 17.

12. The Key Witness

THE prosecution had arranged for two separate trials. We were set to prosecute Bones and Huggins first since both of their signed confessions had been allowed into evidence and would be presented in open court to the jury. We figured that once they'd been found guilty, we'd have paved the way to prosecute Butler and Ramirez together. But the prosecution's best-laid plan was mutilated by legal defense maneuvering and delays designed to fog memories and put victims like me on an emotional roller coaster with no end in sight.

These kinds of legal maneuvers are often utilized by defendants, who could fire their public defenders over and over again, thus delaying trials for years. These creeps had been good at choreographing delays, something they managed to arrange four or five times and I wondered if they could keep doing it until I was old and gray. Finally, though, unable to put it off any longer, they arranged for Butler and Ramirez to be prosecuted first. This meant that my neighbor, in whose house we took shelter, could not testify because he would be out of the country on the court dates. I never understood why my boss Brad didn't testify, since he had witnessed firsthand my state of mind immediately following the crime. But they didn't even think to call him in until I mentioned it for the second trial. By then it was too late; the damage would already be done.

As the key witness, I could not watch the proceedings, but my brother Dave was present for all of it, starting with opening statements. He didn't tell me what they'd said or what the defense had up their dirty little sleeves, for fear of upsetting my fragile state of mind, and I didn't ask. I just wanted to get it over with and send the bad guys to jail so we could regain a sense of control. I craved to remember what life was like when we thought the world was safe.

It felt like someone was playing a legal chess game with me, the victim, as the pawn. Cameras rolled during those difficult days as reporters furiously jotted notes for their evening reports, featuring the sordid details. But they were not really the details at all. Rather, they wrote fabricated versions of the crime as presented by the defense. This was pretty juicy stuff and although it was not the truth, it definitely got people's attention.

•   •   •

OPENING statements ended on that Friday afternoon, with everyone prepared to return on Monday to begin testimonies. I awakened on Saturday morning to a gorgeous sunny day in San Diego. A slight haze hung in the pale blue open sky and I peered through the black wrought iron bars on the hotel window. Below, on the pool terrace, Dave, currently "the snorkeling instructor," was teaching his son Shawn and Breea to dive to the bottom of the pool. Then he showed them how to come up to the surface with a furious blow, spouting water into the air. I laughed to see my daughter's tiny face so dwarfed by her snorkeling equipment that only her eyes were visible. She waved at her uncle Dave, carefree and excited to be playing with him and her cousin. I would join in the festivities and get this weekend off to a good start, leaving everything else behind while I cooked a hearty breakfast for everyone.

I got in the car with my long grocery list, feeling so lighthearted, I hummed a tune to myself as I drove down the long paved road in the direction of the nearest supermarket. I walked inside and headed for the newsstand. It had been a long time since I'd cared about what was going on in the world, particularly San Diego, and I took it as a good sign that I actually wanted to read a newspaper.

I picked up the *Union Tribune* and froze when I read the headlines: PROSECUTORS CALL ROBBERY "NIGHT OF TERROR" BUT DEFENSE SEES "NO KIDNAPPING."

No kidnapping? *WHAT?* I wanted to scream at the

top of my lungs. Fighting the urge to run, I read a quote from the defense's opening statement: "There was no kidnapping, folks. The bank manager was no victim. She orchestrated the entire crime, was having an affair with the defendant Christopher Butler and is responsible for the theft of $360,000!"

I caught my breath and read on. I was being accused of masterminding the crime, plotting my daughter's and my kidnapping! I was being blamed for the explosives strapped to our bodies that tormented us still, accused of trying to steal money from my own bank. That was all terrible news to me. But the worst part was that Christopher Butler and his attorney were accusing me of having an affair with him! They knew it was a lie. What about the confessions? How could they be allowed to do this?

Now I understood why Dave had been so careful to say nothing about opening statements. He knew the defense was trying to involve me in the crime. I looked up from the newspaper numb, disoriented, and outraged. It seemed like my brain had been short-circuited and I hardly knew where I was. I couldn't locate the door of the market as everything around me started shrinking, closing in until I was so claustrophobic; it was all I could do to breathe in and out.

A woman walked up to me.

"Are you all right?"

It must have shown on my face. "How do I get out of here?" was all I could say.

"What can I do for you?" she asked.

"Just show me how to get out of here, please."

The woman pointed and I walked on shaky legs toward the door. I could feel everyone watching me. After I got to the car, I leaned out the driver's door and threw up in the parking lot. I spit out the remains of my utter disgust from my mouth and headed for the hotel, with no groceries.

Dave knew something was wrong the minute I entered the hotel room. Breea was taking a shower when I handed him the newspaper that I'd unconsciously taken with me. Now they could accuse me of petty theft, too.

He read it and looked at me with so much empathy, it brought tears to my eyes, and to his. He exhaled. "I didn't tell you because I was afraid of your reaction," he told me quite honestly. I understood. "Strap yourself in for the fight of your life," he said with his arms wrapped around my shoulders. *Don't let go or I'll fall apart,* I wanted to say. But I just squeezed as hard as I could, took a deep breath, and began to feel the fury rising up in my spine.

The weekend I had anticipated with so much relish had taken a turn in a dark direction. Now the best I could hope for was to just get through it. I held on to my daughter all night long, while she slept beside me. I didn't close my eyes once.

B REEA and I wandered into the hotel coffee shop early the next morning. Feeling restless and bleary from lack of sleep, I ordered a large mug of black coffee, juice for Breea, and a couple of waffles.

Lies about me were smeared across front pages of all the local newspapers. I imagined phoning every reporter in the area, telling them the real truth about what really had happened. I was struck by the power of the printed word; if it was printed, it had to be true. If they would just print the truth, maybe people wouldn't believe the lies.

I needed to talk to the district attorney right away, I decided, and take him to task for allowing the bad press. When I got him on the phone, he sounded sympathetic, but not surprised or outraged. "A trial," he explained, "isn't about the truth. It's about gamesmanship and admissible evidence. Truth usually isn't admissible. Michelle, this is like a game of chess, the winner takes all, and the better player doesn't always triumph. Who ends up winning in the end is anybody's guess."

"Gamesmanship?" I exploded at him. "You've got to be kidding me. This is my life we're talking about here!"

He reiterated in his quiet, confident way that our legal system isn't fair, especially for the victims. During my research period, I'd learned about a statute called The Victims' Bill of Rights, supposedly created to help the victim in a violet crime. But it might as well have been written on toilet paper, I thought, it had made so little impact on the real world. The truth was that criminals in this society were treated like royalty compared to victims.

"A prosecutor," the DA told me, "learns to live on a diet of antacids to keep all that garbage from tearing out his guts as he works in a façade called 'for the people,' known as the criminal justice system." I realized that the plight of the prosecutor was his need to buy into the deplorable injustices that took place every day in the court systems, to chew on them and swallow them without throwing up. His battle was to get evidence allowed into court as he held the burden of proof on his shoulders.

"Remember when investigators and Mr. Barend were pressing you for answers to the same questions over and over, even questions you didn't see as relevant?" he asked. "We all knew what was coming and we had to see if you could withstand the thrashing. The dichotomy here is that we have such a powerful case against them, their only recourse is to attack you, so get ready for more. They have no choice. It happens all the time. They call it 'dirtying the victim,' Michelle. In this case, since there are no cops to dirty because of so much physical evidence, you're all they have."

"Dirtying the victim," I repeated. "This is ludicrous!"

He agreed with me, but there were no laws to stop it. In fact, the defense had no burden to prove their false claims or produce evidence that might support their lies. They were energized and ready to fight, like a bunch of hungry pigs greedily rolling around in the dirt in which they rubbed the victim's nose. I had no choice but to move forward with the trial as planned, with less trust in the system than I had when we started.

Once I'd seen the newspaper article that accused me of participating in the crime, Dave stopped trying to save me from the truth, and his observations tumbled out. He described in detail the cast of characters who had been called by the defense to sit in the witness chair. The jury had heard testimony from fellow "gangbangers," and a young black girl named Princess, who was related to the dirty threesome. It came out later that she pimped younger girls for cash in a raunchy ghetto section of the city, reporting back to the others and giving them percentages for their protection.

The court had also heard from Lisa's babysitter who had overheard the plans to kidnap us. After they divvied up the money at her place, she was paid off with a pile of cash to stay quiet. But when she was threatened with jail for not turning in her "friends," she flipped on them and became a witness for the prosecution. In the end, she pled guilty to being an accessory after the fact and spent three months in jail. During her testimony, Dave learned that the same babysitter had reported to Lisa Ramirez and Christopher Butler that their safe had been stolen while they were back in Atlanta just days after the crime. Whether it was actually stolen or if she or someone she knew hid it was anyone's guess. The whole lot of them were twisted and dishonest, out for themselves even if it meant turning on one another.

I was appalled to see this in action. No matter their part in the conspiracy or their failure to stop it, they would get away scot-free or with minimal jail time. When I thought about it, I could not fathom the fact that Ramirez, a mother of three, could have agreed to participate in a crime against a single mother with a daughter. Defense witness scum kept coming and going, Dave told me, with each person more disreputable and despicable than the last.

Finally, it was the prosecution's turn.

DAVE would get up each morning, dress in his business clothes, hug me good-bye, and head to the courthouse. I was grateful he was still allowed to be there, because he nearly had blown it by approaching the lead defense attorney the day of opening statements. Dave walked over to the man who had just taken a seat next to a young, hungry reporter and extended his hand. The man stood to shake hands as Dave held his in a death grip. "I'm Dave, Michelle's brother," he said.

The defense attorney tried to free his hand from the human vise without success.

Dave squeezed tighter and pulled the man within an inch of his face and said, "My sister is innocent and you know it. How can you do this to her? You should be ashamed, you complete dirtbag. How do you sleep at night? How can you live with yourself?"

The man didn't speak and Dave let go of his grip. Then he stepped backward, turned, and made his way out of the courtroom and into the elevator. Close behind him, though, was Detective Rudy Zamora. The elevator doors closed and it was just the two of them. "She needs you in that courtroom. Dave," Zamora said. "You have to keep your cool in there. You have to be strong and stay calm. Do it for Michelle. She needs you more than ever. I know this is tough but we can't let you back in there if you can't hold it together."

After lunch Dave returned to the courtroom and sat quietly next to a young reporter who was practically salivating over the salacious details that I would only learn about later. The elated newsman was prepared to slant his articles in the direction of the criminals for one reason only—it was lurid, and lurid sold papers.

13. Day One

"DID Michelle lift her shirt to show you the dynamite taped to her body and tell you to write down any clues that might be on them in the vault?" The prosecution was questioning Maria, my coworker, and Dave told me everything when he got back home.

"Yes, she did." She clutched a tissue in her fingers. Then she said, "There's no way Michelle would ever be involved in anything like this. She adores her daughter and she loved her job."

The prosecutor looked directly at the jury and stated, "Would she have done such a thing if she had any idea the dynamite was not real?"

"Never," said Maria. "She was completely freaked out and shaking when she told me about Breea in the closet. She said she and Breea would die if she didn't do what the kidnappers told her to do. I've never seen her like that. She is always so happy and positive, you know? But that day she was different, like she was in a trance."

After she had assured them that I was a great boss, she described the terror she felt when she first saw the dynamite. She even cried.

"That's all Mrs. Gonzalez. Thank you."

Other employees were called to the stand and they all agreed that I'd always treated them well and that I had not been acting normally that day. They had all noticed that I looked distracted and frightened and they agreed that I would never have acted like that on my own. Each employee, in his or her own words, said that I had always protected them and that I would never in a million years have involved Breea in anything that was the slightest bit unsavory or dangerous. They knew she was my entire world, and that being a good mother to her was my first priority.

Last on the prosecution witness list before my turn was Allison, my ex-roommate. I'd seen her only once, right after the crime, and now it was two years later. We had moved in different directions in our lives and had deliberately avoided each other. I guess our friendship was one more casualty of that night because when I e-mailed her and suggested we see each other, she hadn't responded. Now that night of horror had driven a permanent wedge between us.

The truth was that I'd never stopped caring about Allison and I worried about her drinking. I had felt somewhat betrayed by the way she had toyed with these men when Breea was in trouble. I'd eventually forgiven her for her selfish behavior but we had never talked about anything. Now I was concerned about what the defense might do to her on the stand. She'd been heavily intoxicated that night and had angered the men so much, I feared their attorneys would take it out on her. She was one of those people who were tough on the outside, but inside, she was fragile, with her own demons from a difficult past. I loved her children, I wanted them to be all right and I hoped the scummy lawyers on the other side would not dissect her like they intended to do with me.

When her testimony was over, she came into the witness room for some fresh, cold water. I could see that she was badly shaken and she barely looked at me. But her sister, who followed her with tears in her eyes, said, "They're going to thrash you, Michelle."

Allison finally looked at me. "Be strong," she said, hugging me. She felt tiny in my arms and she walked out looking relieved that her day in court was over.

Mine, on the other hand, was not. Waiting in that dingy room all alone with my thoughts was no easy task, but it didn't compare with the agony of walking into the courtroom. When the bailiff came to get me, anxiety pains shot from my chest down my arms and into my fingers. I walked into the room to find all eyes on me. It felt like I was about to deliver a eulogy at a funeral.

I was dressed ultraconservative in a rose plaid suit, DA's orders which would further accentuate the criminals' shabbiness in their button-down shirts and ties. Lisa wore a conservative black dress and I wished the jury could have seen her and the others the way I remembered them, masked, armed, and aggressive.

I raised my right hand. "The truth, the whole truth and nothing but" was exactly what I intended to tell, but I was painfully aware that the truth would not be as readily accepted as I originally had thought. "So help me God," I said, finishing my pledge. I pondered the irony that in a system where the truth seemed to have so little meaning, it started with an oath.

When I sat, my mind was filled with advice from friends, therapists, and attorneys. Breathe, they had said, sip water and ask for breaks whenever you need them. The wooden chair felt rigid and the attached microphone seemed to be angrily pointing at my mouth. I noted a pitcher of water, a glass, and a box of Kleenex tissues. I slowly filled the glass halfway with water, cleared my throat, and wondered why my head felt too heavy for my neck.

I turned my head to the left, trying to loosen up my neck, and I inadvertently locked eyes with Christopher Butler. They were as bloodshot as they'd been before, as if he were on heavy drugs or had stayed up all night, or both. He looked right at me with those rheumy eyes the way he did before, ruthlessly. This time I didn't look away. I eyed him sternly without blinking, determination welling up inside of me. The falling sensation in the pit of my stomach eased a little as I felt my strength.

Suddenly, as I continued to look at him, Butler's expression was pleading, as if he wanted my sympathy. He wasn't getting it. I shifted my gaze to Lisa Ramirez, his supposed girlfriend. How could any woman, any mother do such a thing? The rage burned in my gut, my resolve hardened, and I nodded to the prosecutor. I was ready to do what was necessary to bring closure to this terrible phase of my life. I looked at the friendly faces staring at me, drawing strength from Dave and Kristi, sitting side by side in the first row.

I held a picture of Breea in my hands as if to have her right there in that chair with me. The defense, who noticed the photo clutched in my palm, asked that I give it up, stating that my holding the photo was an attempt to sway the jury. I turned my head to the right to see enlarged 11 x 14 pictures of the criminal's mug shots. My stomach lurched when I saw a second-grade picture of my daughter prior to the crime.

Tom Manning placed it in front of me. "Can you tell the jury who this is?" he asked in a serious, deliberate tone.

"That's my daughter, Breea."

"Ladies and gentlemen of the jury, take a look at this photo of a bright and beautiful little girl—an innocent seven-year-old child who was robbed of her innocence and tormented by the defendants sitting in this courtroom." He held the picture in the air, Exhibit 72A. Another photo of her taken after the crime showed a replica of the dynamite taped to her body. It

immediately brought tears to my eyes. If Tom was trying to get me to open up emotionally right out of the
gate, it was working.

Comparing the photographs of Breea side by side,
it was visibly noticeable that she looked tired and
wiser than before, not so soft, innocent, or frail. I
wished to God she had not been forced to grow up so
soon, but there was nothing I could do. Pictures of evidence and the actual physical evidence were presented next, including things that the men had taken
from my home and the guns they had used to frighten
us.

I nearly gagged when I saw the dreaded masks, the
money straps, and one of the stacks of hundred-dollar
bills that I had removed from the vault. The jury was
shown pictures of the boot prints that the detectives
had lifted from my bathroom tiles. They also had revealed to the jury the paint the men had used to color
the pseudo sticks of dynamite to make them look real,
along with the colored wires and tape they'd used to
strap the explosive to our backs.

They presented safes containing some of the stolen
money and a single kinky hair they had extracted from
the back of my Jeep. DNA tests were not done, however, because there was no question of mistaken identity with such overwhelming evidence. One of the
most incriminating pieces of evidence shared with the
jury was a fingerprint they'd lifted belonging to Butler.

I kept wondering when Ramirez's confession
would be read to the jury, but they never saw it. The

judge let it be suppressed because it implicated Butler and, unlike the others, he had not confessed. What they did see were blown-up aerial photos of my house tacked on a corkboard beside larger-than-life black-and-white mug shots of the three men and Lisa. I trembled on the inside, but I remained steely on the outside, determined to show the jury exactly what had happened to us and how much we had suffered.

I managed to remain stoic during my questioning—until they showed me a picture of the closet in which Breea had been imprisoned. No amount of deep breathing or water sipping helped. The room pressed in on my chest and I could hardly breathe. "Please, please Judge. Can I take a break?" I asked through my sobs. I'd been sitting there testifying for three and a half hours.

She hit the gavel. "We'll take a ten-minute recess," she announced. She retired to her chambers as the jury was escorted into their private room. I stumbled down from the witness stand, upset with myself that I'd lost control. In a minute, I found myself back in the witness room, a place I had come to despise in a very short period of time.

I tried to pull myself together, but my vision was blurred, my legs were bouncing all on their own, and I couldn't stop tangling my fingers in my hair while I rocked myself back and forth. "I'm okay, I'm okay," I repeated to myself aloud, trying to sit still. I had less than ten minutes to get it together, go back into that awful room, and pick up where we had left off.

Just before I reentered the courtroom, Tom Manning laid a bomb on me. "Butler is trying to protect his girlfriend by claiming that he was having an affair with you," he said. "He says he met you outside a grocery store and you recruited him to help you get out of debt."

I stared dumbly at him for a moment.

He continued, "The break-in, they're saying, was part of your plan and they also say that Breea knew him, that she came out of her room and said 'hi' to him that night. They're implying they were there for a party and that you got a big chunk of the stolen cash. That's their explanation for the whereabouts of the rest of the missing money, some of which we know was stolen from the safe at Cassandra's apartment. She pled guilty to it, but they don't see her as credible. I'm so sorry Michelle."

I felt stinging liquid rise in my throat at the thought of what the defense was trying to sell to the jury. I wanted to remind Manning that according to reports, they had found the creeps in their moment of glory after a trip to Vegas to spend large sums of their heist or returning from Atlanta, a trip paid for entirely in cash, stolen cash. They even had receipts of their jewelry purchases and stereo equipment. Add it up! I wanted to run out of the witness' room and back into court and scream at the entire room, but I was not allowed to speak my mind. According to the prosecution, speaking up would make the jurors not like me.

I looked at Manning desperately, realizing that

there were actually four criminals in the courtroom, counting the two defense attorneys. When I took the stand once again and they produced not a modicum of evidence that the awful man and I were carrying on, I figured the jury would know he was lying. There was no record of a single phone call between us and there existed no pictures of us together, although Butler insisted that he had taken several. No one had ever seen us together or had ever heard me speak of him. My employees were the only ones who had seen us together the afternoon he had come into the bank.

As if that weren't enough, next they started on my financial history. Besides trying to create a relationship where there was none, the defense was to shame me about having filed bankruptcy. They figured they could provide a motive for my participation in the crime, accusing me of robbing my own bank to further my financial stability. The truth was that my total debt was approximately sixteen-thousand dollars when I filed for bankruptcy, a great deal lower than the national average. Since then, I'd made great recovery strides, but even if I hadn't, filing bankruptcy was legal and plenty of people more influential than I had gone that route.

The defense went on to attack my credibility over a bounced check I'd written. It had been a bookkeeping mistake I'd discovered and had paid back in full, but it was just as the prosecution had said. The defense had so little against me and so much against the criminals, they needed to dig deep. One bounced check was hardly a crime, but the attorneys on the other side inferred that placing a stop payment on a check or having one bounce made me a criminal capable of lies, affairs, robbery, and endangering or even annihilating my own daughter's childhood. It was as if they had sharpened their claws and teeth and were heading straight for my jugular. What had happened to "fair treatment under the law?" It was nowhere to be seen in a trial where the defense attorneys were more like piranhas than human beings.

After Manning had finished questioning me, I got thrown to the lead killer fish, defense attorney Herb Weston, a large, flamboyant brute, who was attempting to portray Ramirez's very significant role in the crime as innocent and insignificant. He ranted, he bellowed, while he twisted everything I said into something indecent or downright absurd. He accused me of being so money hungry I would traumatize and torture my own child.

Mark Chambers, the other public defender, was also doing some fancy dancing to defend Christopher Butler. His client already stood convicted of a 1997 bank robbery in Atlanta. I wondered how he had done his previous heist, if he had taken some unsuspecting bank employee and ruined her life. Chambers, Butler's counsel, had a major job on his hands and now he had no choice but to attempt to attack me via my past sexual experiences. No current law stopped him since the Rape Shield Law protections about a victim's past only pertained to rape victims. I was distraught when

I realized that if I'd been raped, I would have been safer, because they would not have been allowed to discuss my sexual history.

"Tell us Ms. Renee," he started, "you've been with a black man before, haven't you?"

"OBJECTION!" Tom Manning bolted to his feet and shouted. "May we go to sidebar, Your Honor?"

A heated discussion ensued at the left side of the judge's desk. When we returned to the proceedings, that last question had been stricken from the record. But I knew, as did so many victims who came before me, you couldn't unring the bell. That comment could not and would not be stricken from the juror's minds.

Before I went home for the day, Tom Manning, Jeff Higgins, Rudy Zamora, and the detective who had worked so hard to bring these people down, met with me. They wanted to apologize once again for treating me so harshly during the gathering of evidence. "We knew they would take you apart," Rudy explained for the hundredth time. "We had to know if you could survive what the defense was about to do to you. We hope you know that we never stopped believing in you."

I looked from one face to the next. These were the men who had worked diligently for more than two years on this case, trying to make the world a safer place for citizens like Breea and me. Each and every day, they got up in the morning, gulped down some coffee, and hit the streets to clean up the human trash and fight their way through an ever-mounting heap of pro-prisoner red tape. They were heroes of the first order and, as hard as this was, they were helping to restore and heal my broken world. In that moment, I realized they were my champions, not my enemies, and it was important never to forget it.

14. Motives

DAY two wasn't any easier than day one had been. "No more newspapers, Michelle," Dave said as he grabbed the local paper from my hands the next morning in my hotel room. "I can't let you do this to yourself. Now, come on, let's get some coffee."

"Yes, sir!" I said, saluting and getting ready to leave the hotel.

The idea that people were reading trash about me made me feel ill, but the only thing to do was get it over with. We went to the hotel coffee shop, downed plenty of strong black coffee, and then I waited outside for my ride to the courthouse. By the time an undercover detective picked me up in an unmarked SUV, I had my game face on.

"You're doing great," Tom encouraged me when we arrived at the courthouse, and so did Jeff. "Just keep your answers short and to the point," they told me. "Don't give them anything extra that might spark their imaginations. Just 'yes' and 'no' answers. Okay?"

I nodded. "I think I can do that," I said.

But I couldn't. With each intrusive question the defense attorneys asked, I wanted to stand up, point my finger at them, and say, "Listen jerk, I'm the victim here, not the criminal, you rotten merciless bastard!"

Of course I couldn't do that, but I reverted to arguing when I felt cornered. That was not a good plan and, during a recess, Tom tried to reason with me. "Don't argue with them. Michelle. You know the truth, we know the truth, and so does the jury. Just give them clear direct answers and you'll be fine. You can do it!"

I faced the defense once more, trying to stay even and unaffected. "Isn't it true you knew the dynamite was fake?" asked Mr. Chambers.

"No, that is a lie," I answered.

"Isn't it true you drove up the driveway and put some of the money in the bushes for yourself?"

"No, that is also a lie."

Herb Weston, the obese attorney who I felt was out to get me, was in the habit of raising his arm in the air and shouting things like, "Isn't it in fact true that you orchestrated this heist, Ms. Renee? You needed the money didn't you? You engaged in a sexual affair with Mr. Butler and hid the affair from my client, Ms. Ramirez. You in fact know it wasn't my client's voice on the radio that night, don't you Ms. Renee?"

"That is all a lie," I said softly and burst into tears. *Damn! I thought I was doing so well.*

"Do you need a break Ms. Renee?" asked Judge Weber.

I felt defeated, beaten down, and trampled as I faced the stern, kindly-looking woman in robes. "No. I just want it to end. Please can we just get this over with? Please." I wanted to drop to my knees right then and there and beg God, the judge, the defense, and everyone else to make it stop.

By the end of the questioning on the third day, though, I had finally caught on. "Yes," I would say, and "No," I would say next. I had fallen into the very one-word rhythm that my lawyers had encouraged, mainly because I was too exhausted to do anything else. My emotional well had been pumped dry.

I wondered if I were imagining it when I finally heard the defense attorney say to the judge, "No more questions for this witness, Your Honor." I hardly remember getting off the stand and returning to the witness room. I felt exhausted, but also confident, when I left the courthouse that day that the prosecution would win the case. The jury had to be too smart to fall for the lies and false accusation. Didn't they?

The next morning, the last person took the stand— Christopher Butler. I thought it was illegal for the defense to allow their defendant to "knowingly lie." The judge allowed it. I felt that she also allowed information to be presented that should never have gotten past discovery because it was irrelevant, untrue, or unsupported. My attacker was about to take the stand and lie through his teeth. Still not allowed in the courtroom, I stayed at the hotel, trying to recover from being bludgeoned by the defense. Dave reported to me, especially about the surprise arrival of an uninvited guest to the proceedings.

My dad.

For reasons I will never understand, my father had walked into the courtroom unannounced. In his usual inappropriate fashion, he was holding my work resume in his hand and walked straight up to the defense attorney's table and shook hands with the other side. Almost immediately, Tom quickly moved my dad from the "wrong" side of the courtroom, directing him to sit in the back row.

Apparently he and my dad had a few run-ins early in the investigation. No big surprise. According to the investigative team, my dad had called the DA about having information about the case. When they made time to see him at their office, he had no information about anything. He didn't even know where I lived, my home phone number, or what I had been doing with my life since I stopped seeing him years ago. As always, he wanted to be the big shot. Knowing him, he was interested in my moment in the spotlight. Something I dreaded, but that he apparently thought was glamorous.

Tom called me after that initial meeting and asked me, "What's up with your dad?" He could see why I avoided my father at all costs, the little boy in a man's body, vying for attention from anyone and everyone. Tom tried to explain to my father that he was causing me harm that day in the courthouse. Of course he didn't get it, but I had an idea how to get his cooperation.

"Make him feel important," I said.

"Good idea," said Tom. "If we tell him we need him as a potential character witness, he can't stay in the courtroom."

It was settled. They stroked his ego, told him they needed him as a potential witness and ushered him to the witness room. But it was too late. The other side had already used him to their advantage. Just before they asked him to leave, Butler's attorney had gestured to the back of the courtroom at my father and whispered to his client, "That's Michelle's dad sitting in the back."

Butler took the stand, pointed and announced he knew the man sitting in the back of the room, my dad. As the questioning proceeded, Christopher Butler told his made-up story. Of course, he denied stalking me for two long months before the crime, watching me eat, sleep, make love with my boyfriend, take Breea to school, shop at the mall, eat ice cream, and God only knew what else. Instead, he spoke about those times as if he were actually there with us. In his wicked mind, we were an item, lovers, and inseparable.

Dave saw it unfold and could barely contain himself when Butler said, "I know her whole family. Breea woke up when we were partying that night and she wouldn't go back to sleep until Michelle let her say 'hi' to me. We were hanging out, having dinner, and Michelle came up with the idea of my busting through the back door to make it look real."

If I had been in the courtroom, I would have lunged at the man on the witness stand, right after I did the same thing to my father and the defense attorneys. I had so much anger, I felt like I could take them all on. I knew I would never get over how Christopher Butler was capable of such continuous, unsupported outright lies. And what about his attorneys? They were encouraging him with no burden of proof on which to hang their case.

15. The Verdicts

WHEN the jury retired to their deliberation room, the next two weeks would be a hell all its own. I was busy deciding whether Breea and I would return to Alaska to live permanently, or stay in San Diego. I figured she would want to return to Alaska, but when I asked her, I was surprised that she wanted to stay in California.

"I'm a summer girl, Mommy," she explained. "I miss the beach and the sunshine here. And Uncle Dave and Shawn and Nana. Can we stay? Pretty please?"

Oddly enough, I was feeling the same way. I loved California, too, and I resented moving away because of a pack of gang members who were pleased at having ruined my life. Wouldn't it mean they had won if we moved away? I decided we would stay, but we were still frightened to live alone.

Yet again, Dave came to our rescue, offering to move out of his girlfriend's house in Ventura and move himself and Shawn in with us. Things were not going well with his girlfriend and he had been unsuccessful in finding employment in the wireless communications industry.

I took him up on his offer since Breea's and my nightmares went away when he was with us. He had already stayed in our hotel with us during the entire month of the trial phase and once he decided to permanently relocate, we began scouring the local paper for rentals. But possible prospects turned us down for one reason or another, and some of the places we contacted didn't bother calling back. I was anxious because our hotel rental would be running out in a week, which would leave Breea and me homeless. Dave and I prayed on our hotel balcony. I fell asleep that night, still talking to God, and I had a dream.

I was walking through a house with rows of white cabinetry, tile flooring, and a light-colored fireplace, located near the beach. When I awoke in the morning, I called Kristi and told her about the dream. "This is how it always happens with you," she said. "You must have a direct line to God and you're going to find your place Michelle. I just know it!"

After a few calls, I made a 3:00 PM appointment to see a place that we had spotted yesterday from the car. Dave was busy with Shawn and Breea, so I hopped in my car alone and headed to the seashore to meet Mary, the owner of a lovely condo. When I arrived and walked into the small two-bedroom, two-bath condo, I was amazed to see the cabinetry from my dream in the kitchen with the same tiled floor. The fireplace was white, exactly as I'd seen it, so I turned to Mary and told her my story.

Apparently she already knew who I was. There had been so much publicity, that was no surprise, but what she said next was astonishing. "Something is telling me," she said, "to rent this place to you. Don't worry about filling out the application. It's yours if you want it and I'm going to lower the rent by a hundred dollars a month."

I burst into tears, wrote her a deposit, and went straight back to the hotel, thanking God all the way home. When I brought Breea, Shawn, and Dave to see the inside of the place that evening, they were relieved we had a roof over our head. But we were all slightly worried about the size. It was smaller than we had hoped for, a tight fit for sure, but still, it felt right.

"Love grows in small places," Dave said. He knew I was afraid he might bolt after seeing the place.

"Mommy," Breea said, "I like that there are neighbors close by and if something bad happens again they'll hear us this time."

That clinched it. We had found our new home in our old hometown. Now I had something to do instead of pacing back and forth for two weeks of jury deliberations. I could pack up our stuff and prepare to move, hopefully for the last time, while I awaited the fateful phone call telling me to come to the courthouse for the jury verdicts. In fact, the only victim's right that I knew of was the right to be inside the courtroom when the verdicts and the subsequent sentences were delivered. I wanted to be there and we expected them soon, since Ramirez's attorney had been overheard saying there would be a very short deliberation period.

When Tom Manning finally called, I couldn't imagine how "one day of deliberations" had turned into two weeks. Even though it was a financial burden, I'd kept the rental car during the deliberations so I could jump in at any moment and get right to the courthouse. Tom had assured me I would have at least twenty minutes to get there for the news, but once again, the system failed. The phone call I *did* receive on that Friday afternoon was from Tom all right, but he was not directing me to the courthouse. "Michelle," he said, "I'm so sorry to have to tell you this but the verdicts are in and have already been delivered."

What? I stared at the phone for a moment like there was something wrong with it. No one, not even Tom or Jeff had summoned me to hear the verdicts. It was unconscionable. "This can't be happening. What about my rights?" I pleaded.

Learning to trust anyone ever again was becoming more challenging by the second. After everything we had been through, after they had convinced me they believed in me and were on my side, now this. I didn't know who or what to believe anymore.

"We had no time to call and wait for you to get here," he tried to reason with me. "But I'm glad you weren't here." He was talking faster now, trying to placate my obvious rage that must have been steaming right through his end of the telephone. "I really don't know if you could have handled what happened with Lisa."

I held my breath, a terrible numbness spreading through my body.

"She was acquitted, Michelle," he said. "On all charges. She's free to walk the streets. But let's focus on the fact that Christopher Butler, the real bad guy, was found guilty on all charges—except kidnapping you. And there's another trial for the other two coming right up." What he didn't share was the fact that there had been a mistrial declared because of the deadlock and to retry Butler would be too expensive for the state. Tom knew I would make a lot of noise about it and so I didn't know the facts for months. I was told he was found not guilty.

"What do you mean he was found not guilty of kidnapping me? What the hell else would you call it?"

Tom paused a moment. "One woman juror believed that the two of you had an affair and she was the last standout," he said. "The jury hung on four of the counts because of that one juror. I spoke to her myself and she said she believed you must have had *something* to do with this. I looked her in the eye and told her that Lisa had confessed. But as you know, her confession was inadmissible and the jury never heard it.

"You're forgetting that Butler and the other guys will be sentenced in a month or so and they'll never see the light of day again. Isn't that enough, that the ringleader is being taken off the streets?"

No, that was not enough, I thought, when I hung up the phone. It made no sense at all since he'd been found guilty of kidnapping Breea and Allison but not me.

Still, he was going to jail, so why wasn't I ecstatic? I didn't feel the desired release because my rights had been violated again—this time by the people I had just learned to trust. The closure I had so anticipated, the satisfaction of seeing Butler and Ramirez convicted in front of the entire courtroom, the press, and me had been taken from me. How would I have reacted to Lisa's acquittal? I will never know, but I resented the implication that I could not have handled it. I was strong enough to go through the experience and to give my testimony. Where did anyone come off judging me as too weak to follow this through to the end?

At least the monsters were off the streets. But I was intensely disappointed that I'd been denied the climactic ending I wanted. And then, Lisa was as free as I was. It felt like I'd been involved in a winner-take-all chess game and I'd won but I was denied the right to savor the fruits of my hard work. I felt used, not only by the defense attorneys, but also by the entire justice system. It was just so hard to accept. I'd behaved like they'd asked, dressed as they had suggested, and cooperated in every way. Now that we had basically won our case, I felt like they were done with me. They weren't even going to retry Butler on the four counts for kidnapping me, conspiring to kidnap me, aggressively assaulting me, and burglarizing my home. It just wasn't worth it.

Two days later, I stared stonily at a picture of Lisa Ramirez on the front page, hugging her sister. The caption read: "Set free and acquitted on all charges: Lisa Ramirez gets a second chance on life."

The article described the trial and even quoted Lisa saying how important her children were to her. Yeah right, I thought. So why did she keep them in a house rumored to be infested with drugs while she plotted crimes against innocent women and drove her man to the scene with her children in the backseat? How dare she call them "her first priority"? She would never understand a mother like me who actually *did* make her child her first priority.

Did Breea and I get a second chance on life? No, we had to deal with this for the rest of our lives and Lisa Ramirez was free. At the end of the article, they even mentioned her confession, but it didn't matter anymore. I was too enraged and disillusioned to care.

Now it was trial time for "Big Hershey" and "Bones." August 30, 2002, was when I saw the headlines that read ROLE OF BANK MANAGER IS RAISED IN ROBBERY TRIAL. I was already too numb to react. I had lost all hope of real justice, and when I took the stand for the second time, I steeled myself against the next set of public defenders who were ready to bash me like the first. During the second trial, however, the jury had heard their confessions and there was no way to implicate me. In fact, they never mentioned me during their admissions of guilt. My boss took the stand in the second trial as well (after I suggested it) and so did our neighbor who took us in that morning. After I testified for six hours, the jury deliberated for one day. This time I was there for the reading of "guilty on all counts." I felt a sense of triumph, but it was bittersweet.

16. Victim Impact

I was a loaded gun, cocked and ready. I couldn't wait to look him square in the eyes. Walking hand in hand with Kristi and Dave, I boldly passed the hordes of riffraff outside the courtroom. They had gathered to support the scum that had tried to destroy us. They stared at me hard and cold, as if I'd done something wrong to dismantle their gang family. They wore bandanas, loose pants, and T-shirts. Stone-cold hollow eyes glared at me as I passed through the double doors leading to Courtroom 17. I pitied them. Nothing more. Nothing less.

As I entered the courtroom, I could hear bodies shifting in their seats. Everyone on the right side of the room—family members and friends of the criminals—focused their gazes on me. Little children in braids and bows, sitting beside their parents, scowled at me as if it was my fault that their misguided loved ones violently attacked us for greed money.

When the time came, Judge Joan Weber asked me to step forward. It was my turn to say what I needed to say. Butler sat to my right at the defendant's table with his angry attorney. He stood up just as I was about to step forward, and spoke.

"Is what she has to say even relevant?" the defense attorney asked. "We already know they've been found guilty. Let's just get on with the sentencing."

The judge glowered at him and said, "It's her right to deliver a personal statement about how the crime has impacted her and her child's lives."

He begrudgingly took his seat. There was no way I would be stopped from speaking my mind. I felt as if each time I opened my mouth, I shot out bullets of the truth, with the first one hitting Chambers right between the eyes. I spoke my own words from my heart and from the depths of my wrenched gut with no interruptions. No longer intimidated or afraid of saying or doing the wrong thing, I looked at him boldly and said, "*Everything* I have to say here today is relevant, Mr. Chambers."

After all the tears, terror, and moving from place to place, this was my moment, our moment. I'd labored over my statement, waking up in the middle of the night to add something here and there. I'd read it over a hundred times, making sure I hadn't left out anything crucial. I forgot that all I needed to do was be myself and be brutally honest. I began.

"You three men and Lisa Ramirez didn't just wake up one morning and decide to go inside a bank and rob it that day. No, you premeditated for weeks to commit crimes that would destroy innocent lives forever. You planned the devastation of a seven-year-old girl's childhood. You impregnated our minds with terror in our own home."

I looked squarely into the bloodshot eyes that had haunted me for so long. "You, Mr. Butler, planned this act of terror. You broke down our door with guns loaded with bullets, loaded with greed, and killed us in so many ways. You carried spears, sharp with malicious intent meant for the maiming and mutilation of our animals."

I reloaded.

"Lisa Ramirez should be sitting here with you right now. For reasons I will never understand, her admission of guilt via her signed confession was not presented as evidence in this court of law where there seems to be no room for truth. Consequently, the judge does not have the opportunity to sentence her according to the law and I have to hope that God will punish her fairly and justly in her lifetime."

I'd worked hard on my statement, realizing this was my only chance to speak up on behalf of my daughter and myself. I wanted to take full advantage, hopefully swaying the judge in the direction of the toughest sentences allowable under the law, since these people were clearly a scourge on society. Next, I proceeded to describe to the court what Lisa and these men had done to my daughter.

"My Breea . . . what you have done to the life of this innocent, sweet child is heinous. She was just seven years old, bright and secure, fearless and independent and full of child wonder. You murdered the little girl she once was when you brutally attacked her and terrorized her mother in front of her. When you violently assaulted my daughter you altered her permanently. Imagine what she must have been feeling. Three strangers in black with masks breaking down our door, rushing toward us and one of them chasing her into the bathroom. Viciously manhandling her to the ground, grabbing and dragging her, taping her up while she was facedown on the carpet not knowing what was happening to her mommy. This is what was planned, thought about, and discussed between you three men and Lisa and then you all carried out your disgusting plan."

The gun was smoking. I detailed the irreversible damage they'd done to my precious child, the ruination of her Christmas, her fears to go to the bathroom alone in school, and her inability to join the rest of the class on field trips unless I was there. I talked about her stomachaches, her fear of men, and her inability to sleep.

Then I talked about what the event had done to me.

"As for me, I, too, have lived an absolute nightmare, stalked and plotted against, mercilessly plunged to the ground on my face, tied up and strapped with explosives with guns at my temples. My child ripped from me, a friend's life in the balance, and threats of the disintegration of us all if I didn't do unthinkable things forced upon me by you appalling men. You are vile men who knew details of my life only because you are parasites, existing only to take from others in our society, taking what can never be regained. Watching what should have been private, taking note of where I went, what I drank or ate, who I was with, where my child went to school, premeditating a crime that slaughtered my life as I knew it.

"I live with invisible wounds, without ever being able to forget your voices. I still have flashbacks of your every move and the waving of your guns in my face, the sound of a shattered door, your force to the back of my head. I wake time and time again at night with fear, anxiety, and nightmares. I struggle to trust anyone and question everyone's motives because of you. I jump out of my skin every day from noises surrounding me, loud and scary noises put in my head by you."

My voice was getting louder.

I detailed my sudden vomiting episodes, headaches, pains in my chest, an inability to wear anything around my wrists, and the terrible sexual threats that, thank the Lord, were not carried out. I explained the distance between Allison and me since that night when they ruined our friendship by introducing memories that neither of us could handle when we were together. I did my best to explain my insomnia, the struggle to get up in the morning and face the day with no rest or peace. I talked about our revictimization and how everything in our lives had changed for the worse.

"We no longer have health insurance or the income to pay what it cost. I am unable to afford retraining because school tuition is so expensive and what is available to me through Workmen's Compensation doesn't prepare me for an equal career or the ability to provide for my child and her education or my retirement. You robbed me of my plans, my wages, my dreams and hopes, my life as it was. What you have done will live in me forever, has changed me forever, has changed us forever. There will never be enough time or words to describe all of the pain and irreversible damage you have caused by choosing to commit this senseless, ruthless act of violent crime against us."

I took a great deal of pleasure in addressing the defense team, the group of punishing, critical men who had further terrorized me on the stand.

Cocked and ready.

"Finally, this is for the defense attorneys who were nothing less than cruel to me, particularly Herb Weston and Mark Chambers. It is beyond my comprehension why knowingly speaking lies in a court of law isn't against the law. Why aren't you all being disbarred for your vulturelike tactics against someone whose life you knew had already been massacred by violence and terror? You knew we were already shattered into a million pieces and you knew the truth. You knew we were innocent, raped of our lives, our security, our safety, our trust, and our home, our every-thing, even our spirits for a time. You read the confessions and still you recklessly, without care, stabbed and stabbed and stabbed until I was bleeding to death in here. What you did to me in this courtroom was criminal and I hope someday you will have to answer for it."

I elaborated on the victimization and pleaded with the judge for the maximum sentence.

"I have been praying for the judge to find it in her heart to impose the maximum time allowed by law so that these men may find remorse. Imposing the maximum sentence is fair and just and the only hope we have of justice being served for what has been done to us, to our lives. Please don't let them walk our streets ever again because they chose their actions and should be accountable and responsible for their premeditated behavior."

I went on to thank the prosecution team and I closed with a statement from Breea that she had asked me to read. It deeply affected everyone in the court-room:

"Breea wrote this and asked that I read it to the court:

You made me so afraid of the darkness, so afraid of nighttime, so sick to my tummy with really bad stom-achaches all the time and afraid something is going to happen to my mommy whenever she goes any-where and I get so scared. I don't like people as much anymore because I think they might hurt us

like you did. My nightmares have been so bad and I
still miss all my friends I used to have. I hope you go
to jail for such a long time so you can't hurt anyone
ever again and mess up everything like you did to us.
But I will keep praying with my mommy that people
like you get better inside your heart.

There was not a dry eye in the courtroom. When I sat down the judge spoke swiftly and to the point. "For this woman to go through everything you men put her through, for her daughter to be left for dead and then have to come in here and be attacked again in our court of law is unthinkable. Mr. Butler's testimony is an outrageous pack of lies." She sentenced them all to the maximum time allowable under the law: Three life sentences plus sixty-four years.

17. Confessions

My car was still in Alaska. So were most of our things. Breea and I took to the sky once again. This time, it was not about running away from anything.

Just as the Alaskan frontier had healed us before, by the time our plane landed, we already felt released from defense attorneys, prosecutors, newspaper reporters, and glaring strangers. It was a welcome reprieve.

I had hoped to rent a U-Haul but we were still in a financial crunch so we loaded up the small Kia Sportage with whatever it could hold. A few days later, we packed up the last of our stuff, ready to roll out of town the next morning. I had just gone into the house for the last armload when the phone rang around 4:00 PM.

The last thing I expected was good news. It had been a long time since I'd had any. But my spirits soared when the man from the Social Security office said, "We've approved your claim and we have a check for you that includes eleven months of back pay. Can you stay here until Monday and pick it up?"

Can I stay? "Absolutely!"

We got the check on Monday morning and by early afternoon, we rolled out of town pulling a U-Haul. It was carrying everything we owned, including the new bike Breea got from her dad for her birthday, and my old mountain bike. I got a map and planned the road trip of a lifetime for us. We didn't have to be anywhere at any particular time. This time the trip was for us and us alone.

We traveled from Alaska through the mountains of Canada to the West Edmonton Mall, a fabulous place where we sailed down slides in a gigantic indoor water park. We went horseback riding and white-water rafted in Montana, and finally drove through the magnificent beauty of the Redwoods where I had so hoped to bring Breea someday. We were learning more about each other and about ourselves, discovering how to enjoy life again.

We traveled through small towns and the Grand Tetons. We walked on beaches and waded in rivers. We traveled highways and dirt roads that tossed up rocks that shattered our back window to smithereens. It didn't matter. We loved it all. After twenty-four incredible days on the road, this time staying in bed-and-breakfasts instead of tents and eating cold canned suppers, we fell asleep with hope.

By the time we arrived home, we had a brand-new lease on life, a new start, and new dreams to pursue. But first I had to know, really know, what went on in the interrogation rooms when all four suspects had been arrested. I knew they had confessed, all but Butler. But what had they said? Who were these people? I had to know. What I didn't expect to find was more red tape. It seemed to envelop the entire judicial system, a perverse sort of conspiracy to keep victims in the dark.

I was told I would have to pay through the nose for court transcripts or any other documentation concerning the case. The paperwork belongs to the state and I had never seen my tormentors' confessions or the transcripts from the trials. I wanted access to all of it now, especially since the three men had been found guilty. Due to my imposed courtroom absence, I had gaps in my mind concerning their testimony. I wanted to know firsthand exactly how badly they had lied in court. It was my privilege to know.

But when I finally discovered that for a price, I *could* get my hands on them, I didn't have the thousands of dollars it would cost to purchase them. My reasons for wanting the transcripts were threefold:

First, to understand what these misguided, angry people had been thinking when they planned the crime. What made them tick? Did they really think they could get away with it?

Second, to know the real truth "and nothing but the truth" about what had happened in court. I was feeling a great deal of mistrust after the "good guys" had failed to summon me to the courtroom to hear the verdicts of the first trial.

Third, so I could model victim programs the right way. For this, my commitment had only grown stronger over the past several months. My continuing research as well as my personal experiences had shown me that violent criminals were the prima donnas of our justice system and it simply wasn't right. Those of us at the receiving end of such crimes were treated with cruelty under the guise of the premise, innocent until proven guilty. Under the current system, the victim got bashed first and then underwent a series of subsequent bashings at the hands of the justice system.

I had been stunned to discover defense attorneys were allowed to deploy punishing and vulgar tactics toward the wounded, like slander and defamation of character. There was so much that I didn't know and I was intent on educating myself.

A few days after I started calling (and begging) for the signed confessions, transcripts, and sworn statements, I got a phone call from an anonymous person in the courthouse. "There's a package for you at the front desk on the fifth floor," the male voice said. "But hey, you didn't get these from me."

So, that was how it worked.

I drove over to the courthouse and picked up a manila envelope with the confessions, interrogation interviews, disks of all the photographed evidence from the raids and crime scene, partial transcripts, and the FBI 302 reports that contained notes from the scene when I'd given my statement. I was relieved to finally have the papers, but it was two weeks before I got up the nerve to start reading them. I'd walked past the thick stack of legal paperwork sitting on the coffee table day after day, wondering how I would ever begin.

I wanted to be alone to allow the emotions to surface naturally. One evening after Breea had gone to bed, I fixed myself a cup of hot tea, curled up in the corner of my sofa in my comfortable sweats, tucked my feet beneath me, and began to read.

I started with Lisa Ramirez's confession, given nine days following the crime. Hers was the thickest stack of papers, which suggested she had done a lot of talking. So why hadn't the jury seen her confession? I just couldn't get beyond that one. *It's water under the bridge,* I kept telling myself, *and I need to focus on the words in front of me.* Or should I say, the lies.

Page after page of her paperwork contained nothing but elaborate fabrications, like a discussion about Butler, her fiancé. "He came here to start a photography business." I felt my eyes burn when I remembered his card, "On the Spot Photography by Christopher Butler." In fact, I would never forget it. I wouldn't forget his posture, either, or his rheumy, expressionless eyes. Or the way he leered at Breea's picture. I feared I would take these images with me to the grave.

After I'd read about twenty pages of lies and question dodging, I was surprised to find that starting on page twenty-one, Lisa had begun to come clean. Well, not actually *clean*, but she admitted plotting the crime with her boyfriend and said that a friend had snitched on them, hoping to cash in.

The more I read, the more everything began to fit together. "A deputy district attorney," one of the interrogators had told Lisa, "is outside right now waiting for me to tell him how we want to handle this. Why don't you start at the beginning and tell us everything that happened? We'll tell the DA how well you cooperated. We're not making any promises about the future but cooperation always helps."

My head dropped backward on the cushion. According to these papers, a deal was broached in an offhanded sort of way, long before that call to me at the mall. Did they know then that she would walk? Is that why Tom tried to get me to take the plea bargain? Was that why they never showed her confession to the jury and she was acquitted, for her "cooperation"? Nothing surprised me anymore when it came to the way things "worked" in our so-called legal system.

Then I noticed the word "revised" written across the top of Ramirez's confession papers. What did that mean? How could original legal documents containing sworn statements be revised? I should have taken the plea bargain. At least Lisa would have been put away for twelve years. Now she was free, at least physically.

I was disappointed that the prosecution team, supposedly *my* team who *knew* I had almost no rights, had failed to inform me that I was entitled to a private attorney that day in the interrogation room. But I would have had to pay for one, while the criminals were offered one public defender after another for free. Had I needed my own attorney? I was innocent and ignorant and they knew it. Would my own attorney have helped to make certain that Lisa did not walk?

Surely someone representing my personal interests *should* have been there for me, or at least one should have been offered to me. Maybe that would have stopped the prosecution team from barraging me with questions about my past, my sex life, and everything else under the sun. I was never given the option to have someone there just for me, to protect me from further harm.

Someone should have informed me that the criminals were capable of·holding up the proceedings with elaborate legal maneuvering. Even after Bones and Huggins were found guilty, their sentencing continued to be postponed over and over again. It never had mattered what I wanted or needed. The criminal's rights had continued to overshadow those of the victim every step of the way.

The biggest shock of all was on page nineteen where Ramirez stated: "One thing I have been told is that there was a white lady involved in it. I think her name is Michelle. Supposedly from what they had told me, this Michelle lady was helping them, that basically we were getting hush money. That is what they told me."

The implications of that statement were why the prosecution ripped me to shreds in my initial interrogation. They wanted to prepare me for what her attorney would do to me. And I suspect they wanted to satisfy themselves that there was no truth in her words.

She continued, "I don't know how they met her but they already knew her. I know they told me a lot of personal things, they were kind of joking about her. They said she was a druggie and a nymphomaniac and they said they brought her into the plan that night. She lied to you guys about my boyfriend. She was flirting with my Chris in the bank when we were there."

I cringed at the very idea. Ramirez's personal insecurities obviously had allowed her to get involved with that creep in the first place. After about forty more pages, she cracked. "The only reason I lied was to protect Chris," she suddenly admitted.

Indignation rumbled in my gut. Imagine trying to protect a convicted bank robber who tormented a single mother and her child and their roommate! I didn't get it, but at least she was telling the truth for a change. When I read her words, "I actually do feel better," I guess I began to understand. No matter how malicious she was, if she had even an ounce of decency, the fact that she had helped torment us had to be a heavy burden to carry. I hoped it was.

In the next few pages, I learned that she and Butler had lived together on Avery Street in a house rumored to be infested with drugs and too many people to count. Apparently, a fifteen-year-old girl, a wannabe gangster-rapper, and a part-time underaged pimp, the one called Princess who took the stand at the trial, was living in the garage with the big guy they called Big Hershey. When Butler had run out of money, he and Lisa and her kids had been forced by Cliff, the landlord, to sleep in the living room.

I looked at the pictures of her house that was raided by the police. It was a disgusting pigsty where no child should ever have to live, let alone three of them. Cliff had been part of the original heist plan, which Butler had plotted in August or September. He had been cut out of the deal (apparently because of his big mouth) and then testified against them in court: "I told them I didn't know why people didn't just use fake dynamite when they robbed banks, so they took my advice."

I felt a ripple of self-pride that I had been right about Ramirez devising a part of the plan, one that significantly terrorized us. How sick could she be? I read about how they had made the dynamite look real, including a "penny roll" they placed under the tape to make the false explosives look capable of detonating. They had done such a good job on the dummy dynamite that the bomb squad detectives couldn't rule out its authenticity from three feet away.

I looked up from the papers, breathless. Shots of pain traveled from my neck and down my arms from sitting in the same position too long. I stood up and stretched, warmed up my tea, and settled back in for more. Lisa described driving them to my house and she said that Bones had provided the two handguns. She said when they'd first arrived at the house the night before the crime, our dogs had barked so loudly they'd taken off. I recalled the coyotes and dogs on the block that had begun baying and shrieking. The thing was, they did that so often, it was hard to determine if there was actual danger, or if they were merely howling out to their pack with the dogs responding.

So Breea had been right. There *were* people outside her window when she'd come running to me that night. I owed her an apology for dismissing her fears the way I had. But if I'd listened and called the police, could we have avoided the worst experience of our lives? Probably not, but I felt awful for having doubted my daughter for even a second.

As I read on, I discovered that the guys' lack of success the night before the crime had almost caused them to dissolve their plan. The dogs could easily get in their way, but because Bones had a dog of his own, Voodoo, they decided to use him the next night to distract our dogs. If it didn't work, they had their spears (the FBI called them "stabbing devices") as a backup so they could kill our dogs without sounding a gunshot that might alert the neighborhood.

The next evening, the night when the actual crime occurred, Lisa had dropped them off again. This time things had gone better for them. Then I noticed something extremely disturbing on a page of the FBI 302 reports. There was my original statement to the FBI at the neighbor's house when I said I'd recognized Lisa's voice on the two-way radio as the woman who had been in my bank. But my detailed description of the crime and who was involved never made it to the grand jury trial. In fact, by the time Joe Barend, the prosecuting district attorney, suddenly retired and Tom Manning took over the case, the very important fact that I had recognized her voice had gotten lost in the shuffle. Now, right here, Lisa Ramirez herself had admitted, "The voice on the other end of the radio was mine." Wouldn't that information have made the jury think twice about letting her walk free?

It seemed that Ramirez, in her state of paranoia, actually had believed that by the morning of the bank heist, I had made friends with these men.

Right, I thought, meet my new buddies with masks and spears and an intention to torture my daughter. It was so ludicrous I almost laughed when I read, "They told me they were going to intimidate her but then they said they hadn't had to do that. She just went right along with it and did everything they asked her to do. I heard music and stuff. He made it sound like they were having a good time over there."

Did she call being strapped with explosives and having our lives threatened "a good time"? The bottom line was that Lisa had made up a fairy tale for the first part of her testimony, but her insecurity and paranoia showed up in the rest. She said that her fiancé had told her that I'd taken a cut of the money. "And I never saw a dime of it," she complained. "Isn't that ironic?"

It was almost comical. She made up such ridiculous tales, using their infantile shortwave radio code names: Money One, Two, Three, and Four. They were not particularly creative, but I had to admit that the names pointed to what mattered most to these people.

She went on about fearing Bones, described this friend of her fiancé's as "a weird-looking guy who wore his hair in thick braids." He was shadier than the rest, she had said, with tattoos on the neck and arms of his emaciated body. She described a hungry look in his eye, as if he were a crack junkie. That unstable, trigger-happy man was the one they put in charge of my daughter that night.

At this point in the transcripts, it was noted that the door to her interrogation room had swung open. An agent had walked in, telling Lisa that her boyfriend was spilling everything in the next room. He wasn't. It was all part of their game, and she retold the story again from the beginning, with very few differences from her first version. She admitted that they took about three thousand dollars with them for a trip to Atlanta for the Thanksgiving holiday, the worst holiday of my life. They left the rest of the money at the babysitter's house in a safe they'd purchased at Wal-Mart. But when the babysitter, Cassandra, by then in cahoots with the FBI, told them on the phone that the safe had been stolen (which it had), they'd rushed back to town and were arrested.

I felt a smile form on my lips. I listened to the soothing sound of trickling water from the stone fountain in my living room. I watched the moon shadows dance across the room. I felt sorry for Ramirez's children. I just couldn't help it, and I prayed that somehow they would be rescued from the horrific situation in which they were being raised. I hoped they would someday be transported to good homes with good people who shunned drugs and crime. That was their only chance.

I stretched, yawned, and glanced at the clock. It was 1:17 AM. I was far from finished. I still had the men's confessions to read.

18. Sweet Dreams

I made myself another cup of peppermint tea, went back to the living room, sat on the couch and picked up the next batch of papers. They contained the confession from Huggins, aka Big Hershey, the big guy. His real name was Adams and his stack of papers was less than half the size of Ramirez's. A man of few words, he had no prior felony convictions, had only known Butler for a few months, and was totally protecting him. How did Butler get these people not to rat on him? I recalled a movie *Helter Skelter* about murderer Charles Manson who had gotten his followers to commit unthinkable acts of violence by keeping them brainwashed on drugs.

In Huggins's case, it must have been fear of retaliation since he did not give up Butler until almost the very end of the transcripts. He never mentioned my name or insinuated in any way that I was involved. Rather, he confessed to stealing the items from our house and finally admitted that Butler had made the bombs. Apparently after Huggins got his cut, he'd hightailed it to Vegas, where he blew tens of thousands of dollars on gambling and jewelry for a couple of ex-girlfriends. The FBI had found some of our stolen items still in his car but most of the money was long gone.

I moved on to Bones's confession, which he had given at the very beginning after being pulled from a small crawl space in Milwaukee. I flashed back to his arrest on the news after *America's Most Wanted* had profiled the case. His confession was short and anything but sweet: "As a matter of background," he'd said, "the only individuals involved in the events were myself, a black male named Chris Butler, another black male named Chris Huggins, Butler's girlfriend, Lisa Ramirez, and a female named Cassandra Stokes."

The babysitter. Without messing around or wasting an extra word, he talked right through the entire ordeal, from start to finish. At the end of his statement, he had handwritten the following words: "This statement is simply for all the false accusations against me to be cleared up and not to label no one personally. If anyone feels different then do what you must."

I put down his papers and reached for the last pile of transcripts: those of Christopher Butler. The convicted bank robber and ringleader did not confess. He denied everything. No matter that his fingerprints had been lifted from the explosives, that a hair fiber found in my truck was believed to be his, or that the others had pointed to him in their confessions. He never budged from claiming his innocence. His statement was a mess of contradictions—backpedaling, fantasy, and fabrication. I learned a lot about him as I read, but even more about the justice system. He had previously been convicted of one bank robbery in Atlanta, entered into a plea bargain agreement, and did three years. Imagine! He got three lousy years while the lives of innocent people had been destroyed.

When I looked up, it was 3:00 AM, close to the time our intruders had put on the movie, *The Perfect Storm*. How fitting that I was finished.

I returned the papers to my coffee table and allowed my mind to float. As much as I felt contempt for these misguided individuals that had wreaked such havoc in my life, a small spot in my heart was softening from finally knowing the truth. I wondered if I would ever see human beings in the same way. What made these criminals the way they were? Were they abused when they were young? Was that how they had turned into such bitter, desperate, hostile people?

I lay back against the sofa cushions and closed my eyes.

Bones was from Santa Barbara, in large part a wealthy neighborhood. I wondered how he had ended up so angry at the world.

When Lisa dropped her tough, stone-faced attitude,

you could even call her pretty. What had hardened her to such a degree before she reached thirty years old?

Before the crime, Huggins was caring for the elderly with no prior felony record. Why had he gone along with such a plan?

Then there was Butler, the ringleader. Had he always been sick and twisted? Was he ever cuddly or sweet or romantic or funny? Was it his childishness Lisa fell for? Did she see him as a sweet little boy who needed love? There were no answers, only more questions, but the monsters that had trampled my life were becoming less powerful by the moment. Maybe they weren't really monsters at all. Maybe they'd been thrust into a world of victim/persecutor until that was all there was. Maybe they were told all their lives that they would be nothing and believed it. Who were they really, deep down? What had happened to them? What made them live so close to the edge that they had just fallen off?

I had closed a long and brutal chapter in my life. To relax my mind I sketched a symbolic picture of a woman with her arms wrapped around her pregnant belly, fully embracing what was inside—not a child but her own new vibrant life. I stood and blew out the candles, remembering a promise I'd made to my mother. I would return with her to her hometown and help her complete the healing of her heart. My anger had dissolved as I walked down the hall to my bedroom.

I watched the peaceful rise and fall of my daughter's small chest as she lay asleep in my bed. I fully understand how close we had brushed death. I was grateful to be alive and I dropped to my knees beside Breea's bed. "Thank you," I said to God, "thank you."

I climbed into bed with her, remembering what I had said to Dave so many times before: *it is all about the message.* I kissed Breea's forehead one more time and whispered, "Sweet dreams, my angel. Sweet dreams."

Breea was laughing again. Our life had become a gentler place, and my well-being had come full circle so completely that I began to stop waiting for the right time for things to happen and start living out my dreams. On the morning of May 9, 2004, Kristi and I took the trip I'd been dreaming about my whole life. After dropping Breea off with Dave, we took off in celebration of our friendship, in celebration of adventure and discovery, in celebration of being alive. We landed in Milan, Italy, fourteen hours later. My journey through a painful time took a backseat to our journey through the Old Country. We visited Lake Como, the wineries of Tuscany, the cliffs of the Cinque Terre, explored my Italian roots, and absorbed the amazing history of Rome.

It was sixteen days of bliss, the culture I love, the history that amazes me, the art that fascinates me, the food, the landscape, the wine, the people . . . shared with someone I hold so dear to my heart. As I flew home I could not help but to think about my mom and the way we had bonded on her visit to Alaska. I needed to make good on a promise that I had made to her: to accompany her to her hometown so she could complete her own life story. My mother deserved a happy ending, too.

I committed myself to helping her find it.

19. Finding Finally

BLAME had been holding me hostage all my life, choking out any real hope of discovering my purpose. By my fortieth birthday, I had pulled that deadly weed, roots and all. Now it was my mom's turn.

It's never too late, I thought, gazing into my mom's baby-blue Irish eyes. We stood in the security line at the airport, Breea's hand in mine, ready to board the plane for Niagara Falls in Buffalo, New York, on our way to Maine. It was fall, a perfect time to visit Maine. I hoped Mom could make peace with her past. At any rate, Breea and I would be there, supporting her every step of the way, and I could hardly wait to show Breea autumn in New England. We boarded the plane, three generations of women (well, two women and one young lady) on an adventure.

Niagara Falls was everything I had imagined. I inhaled with a newfound sense of discovery as I stood on the platform overlooking the falls, delighting in the cold mist, the chilly autumn breezes, and the look of awe on my daughter's face. There was so much for her to learn and discover. Thank God she was alive.

We snapped a few photos and cozied up in a warm café, sipping hot chocolate, looking out on the most fabulous view in the world. My mother, never one to open up much and share her innermost feelings, stared blankly. I could see that she was juggling a load of emotions. Her purpose was to find a way to forgive herself for her jaded past, something I wanted my daughter to witness. I'd always imagined a world where forgiveness replaced resentment and now an opportunity lay at my mother's feet.

We rented a car in Buffalo. Feeling strong, I got behind the wheel, happily returning to what I call my "control freak" tendencies. They seemed to have intensified with the crime, probably because I'd felt so out of control for so long. We drove along, Mom gazing out the window, admiring the tree-lined roads, alive in their annual autumn fire dance. It was nice to see her like this, relaxed and in good health. We'd nearly lost her to septic shock from a ruptured tumor just a few months prior to this trip. She'd been in a coma for days, underwent major surgery, and had awoken with a new sense of being alive. She, like me, was beginning her own ascent out of darkness.

I marveled at the colors of nature, the tiny purple and yellow flowers that boldly grew in the cracks between the sidewalks. We passed grand lakes, crossed quaint New England bridges, and admired wide-open fields of dandelions that brought a glow of recognition to Mom's face.

We passed flashes of orange, red, and yellow leaves wafting down from the heavens, forming radiant blankets beneath the naked trees. Once, we stopped and strolled through the fallen leaves, crunching them under our shoes, cupping and crumbling the colors in our hands. As we got nearer to my mother's hometown, I saw that she and I differed in so many ways. Most importantly, her father had been her hero when she was growing up. Mine had been my enemy.

Mom was from one of the wealthier families in the small New England town. She grew up in a large house with eleven rooms on an expensive parcel of land with its own pond. The intensely cold New England winters brought out the annuals in her mother's garden of gladioli. Mom, known for her fiery red hair and unchecked laughter, had been active in her high school in music and drama, living the American dream of the fifties era.

Her dad, the captain of a seventy-seven-foot teakwood and steel sailing schooner, had taken Mom to sea as often as her mother would allow. The vastness of the ocean was my grandfather's passion, something

I inherited as my own. All my life I'd heard about my grandfather, and my mom was his pride and joy until a married man had entered her life. She'd fallen head over heels in love and had flown straight into the arms of "unhappily ever after." She became pregnant with his child toward the end of their six-year affair.

The married man had left her, and Mom had met my dad when my eldest sister, conceived of my mom's affair, was nine months old. It was a vulnerable time for a single woman with an illegitimate child. Dad had said all the right things and although my mother did not feel full-blown passion for him, she loved him and she married him. I marveled that even though she had a loving father, she still had chosen inappropriate men. It obviously had more to do with circumstances than deliberate choices.

As Mom opened up and told me her story, pieces of my own puzzle began fitting together. She talked about my father's brutality and how it had manifested physically and sexually, the extent of which I'd had no real conception. Apparently, the domestic violence squad knew them both much too well, having come out to our house on many occasions. The school, seeing our bruises, had turned us over to child protective services and we were never taken out of the melee since there was nowhere else to put us.

While Breea dozed in the backseat, Mom and I talked candidly about the life in hell we had survived. Her eyes brightened each time she released the burden of her secrecy with another story. We even managed to laugh now and then.

We stopped at stands by the side of the road to buy freshly picked fruit from old-fashioned wicker baskets. Crunching shiny apples and letting pear juice run down our chins, Mom told me about her suicide attempts. I'd seen her bloated body with a large tube and charcoal coming from her mouth lying in the hospital. But now I was learning why she hadn't wanted to live. In the wake of so much naked honesty, I told her about my romantic exploits, the secret six-year love with a man in Cleveland, and my suicidal visions after the crime. I no longer needed to save anyone but myself and I wanted her to know me through and through, the same way I wanted to know her.

When we arrived in Maine, our first stop was the cemetery. After a lengthy search for my grandfather's grave, Breea found the headstone carved with my grandfather's name. I paid my respects to the man I had yearned to know, but had never met. Then I led Breea away, allowing my mom some time alone with her father. She had a lot to forgive and I hoped she would accomplish her mission so she would stop suffering.

I overheard her prayer: "Please know how much I love you," she whispered as she brushed away the leaves from her father's grave, removing twigs and sticks with great gentleness, as if she thought he could feel them. When she left the graveyard, her face shone with a light of forgiveness and surrender.

By the time we left the quaint, seaside town, my mom had reconnected with old friends, gone back to the home of her precious youth, and caught a glimpse of her high school. She told me about the glory days when she had breathed in that familiar, salty fisherman's air. And so, ten days after we arrived, Mom looked and felt like a new woman. Best of all, when we landed back home in San Diego, my mother and I would forever more call each other friend.

This was my final journal entry:

October 7, 2004

My cell phone rang around noon today. It was a newspaper reporter. He wanted to know if I had any comment about the latest developments in the appeals process concerning one of Christopher Butler's convictions, the charge for conspiring to kidnap me. I listened. I gripped the wheel hard and thought for a moment. There was so much I could say. Then I looked at Breea.

This was our time.

"I have no comment at this time," I told the man.

With a smile I glanced again at Breea as I hung up the phone. With our hair blowing in the wind and our favorite music escaping from the speakers, we headed north on coast Highway 101.

We were finally free, with nothing in front of us but the open road and endless possibilities.

Epilogue

WHILE the formerly fearsome cast of characters was taking a backseat in my mind, I tackled the work before me. I was invited to New York to speak and present Lifetime Achievement Awards to two very brave members of the NYPD Bomb Squad. It was their hundredth-year anniversary and the second anniversary of our kidnapping, and Dave was with me. I could not have imagined a better way to change my focus on that date, November 21, into something positive and wonderful and a chance to celebrate Dave's birthday. We began filming employees in crime-targeted industries and college kids on the streets of New York. We interviewed a magnificent man named Richie Pastorella, a bomb squad technician whose face was blown off when a bomb detonated. He knows just how real post-traumatic stress disorder is and spoke

out for our PSA project, PTSD is REAL. I hope to release it nationally someday, as soon as we have the
funding.

Two weeks later, I was stunned to receive a phone
call from Tom Manning.

"I nominated you for the Citizen of Courage
Award."

"Thanks," I said, amazed and delighted.

"And you've been selected," he said. "You won!"

I was amazed that I was being honored by one of
the people I had blamed for Lisa Ramirez's release
and for the treatment I received during the criminal trials. I was determined I would let go of the hard feelings so I could accept my award with grace.

On April 21, 2004, San Diego District Attorney
Bonnie Dumanis presented me, on behalf of the city,
with the Citizen of Courage Award. When she went on
to proclaim that date as Michelle Renee Day in San
Diego, I was embarrassed and overwhelmed to the
point of tears. At that time, I was presented with a letter of praise from California governor Arnold
Schwarzenegger. I was stunned at being honored in
front of more than five hundred prominent business
leaders, some of whom had previously judged and
condemned me. This kind of public validation had
never been my goal. In fact, I would have avoided it if
our organization did not stand to benefit from the attention.

Old pain melted away when I stood at the podium
and appealed to these wealthy, powerful people to use

their good fortune and privilege to support protection of victims of work-related violent crimes. No matter how much I feared being in the public eye, the minute I began my appeal, I felt relaxed and at home. Suddenly it felt as if talking to the leaders of the most highly respected American corporations was the most natural thing in the world.

Three weeks later, I faced the largest Rotarian group in the country, pleading for their support in my fight against violent crime. My goal was to create additional laws to protect victims and give us equal rights and to make sure those laws got passed. The introduction, given by a highly respected businesswoman from the county, was humbling to say the least. She began by telling the crowd how the system had let us down and through it all, I stood up for what was right and what needs to change.

I took the podium and urged everyone to do more for crime victims. At the end of my emotionally charged speech, everyone jumped to their feet, honoring me with a thundering standing ovation. I could finally see what God had in mind for Breea and me. Through an experience of terror, we had reshaped our existence. Not only had we survived; we were living victoriously now. I had found my purpose, something that was missing since long before the crime had happened.

As my life continues to shift from a downward spiral to an uplifting surge of service and accomplishment, I vow to never give up, as Breea has reminded me so many times. To this day, I resort to recalling her strength when the inevitable tests of life unexpectedly show up.

With Breea back in school, my worker's compensation case settled, and issues with my ex-employer resolved, I found some breathing space. I spent hours each day researching PTSD, finding trauma contact information for each state, as well as for resources in other countries. I reviewed each step of the crime against us in my mind, creating lists of what needed to be changed—which turned out to be pretty much everything.

I kept returning to the first line of the Victims' Bill of Rights, which demands "fair treatment" for the victim.

Several months after our tragedy, I'd heard about an unfortunate male pizza delivery employee, also strapped with explosives. His were real. When they found him, they waited forty minutes before they even thought about removing the explosives. They were more interested in determining if he was an accomplice in the scheme.

I guess he got their attention when he was blown to smithereens right in front of them. His last words echoing for eternity: "Why isn't anyone here to take this off of me yet? It's going to blow up. I'm not lying. They set it to a timer." I knew the feeling all too well.

Victims need a load of information, and I was ready to tackle it all, one devastation at a time. I was grateful that Dave had jumped back in, too. We created a list of proposed changes:

- Mandatory time off for a victim following a crime.

- An amendment to the Family and Medical Leave Act that crisis intervention be offered within twenty-four hours of a violent crime and continuing care for those suffering with PTSD.

- A better definition for the term "fair treatment" for victims.

- Protection in court against being attacked by the legal system without a shred of evidence to support false claims.

- Updated security measures, including state-of-the-art surveillance technologies, policies, and procedures, and staff training to deal with potential extortion and kidnapping.

I reviewed the list of necessary victim services: education, awareness, and outreach programs. It was time to get the word out, which should have been easy since every radio station in town had followed my story. I was stunned to discover that even a few weeks after the sentencing, I was old news. I rolled up my sleeves and moved on.

I developed Post-traumatic stress disorder resource materials for crime-targeted industries including a human resource guide and employee information packets. We had trained the victim/witness advocates for the DA's office and were sending out more personal security alarms for victims of physical attacks than we could keep up with. We developed a thirty-day victim recovery program and were enlisting sponsors and members along the way.

Offers began trickling in for me to speak at different venues, inspiring and motivating others to be their kids' heroes and move beyond blame. I began a networking system that led me to wonderful people in different fields of expertise. I addressed college-level criminal justice students at the University of California–Santa Barbara about victimology and PTSD. I explained to them how we, the victims, needed people in their positions to show they cared and guide us to the proper resources, and I reminded them to never lose sight of the victim in their pursuit of the criminal or solving a crime.

My therapist became my partner in educating others about PTSD. We presented my artwork and spoke together at the Eighteenth and Twentieth Annual Children's Hospital Conference on Child and Family Maltreatment. It was a thrill of a lifetime for me to be with her again, this time with her as a part of a team. It wasn't long before businesses asked me to conduct PTSD training for their staffs.

Dave and I pounded the pavement to generate funding for victims. Dave contacted a few faith-based radio stations and soon I was doing radio interviews all across Southern California.

My next stop was Sacramento to introduce my victims rights bill, The Crime Victims Integrity Bill.

"Hey Dave, you won't believe where I am right now."

"Yes I will. Knowing you, it could be anywhere."

"Very funny. I am standing on the steps of the capitol building. I can't believe I am here. When I look back on the past three and a half years I can't help but think how in the heck did I get here? I was just a banker."

"You got there because you are a dynamo, remember? You always tell me it is about the message. Michelle, it really is and it is about the summit. Go kick some butt."

"Thanks Dave. I love you." I hung up and headed straight for the offices of legislators who could help. Within a month I was sitting in a senator's office face to face with a fine supporter of my bill. Then it was off to the Annual Crime Victims Rights Committee meeting I was invited to attend by the California District Attorneys Association.

Today, the Crime Victims Integrity Bill is being shopped around for support from those in government positions who will introduce it in 2007. And I don't intend to stop there.

The Family Medical Leave Act needs major revamping to include the very real and debilitating symptoms of PTSD. Victims need time and resources to process what happened to them and recover.

The Bank Security Act is in need of revision. It was supposedly created to deter robbers and protect liquid assets. We need it to be relevant to today's sophisticated crimes.

Breea got involved too, telling her story to kids her age and encouraging them never to give up in the face of adversity. In fact, those were her words, which birthed the Girls against Crime Club.

I was presented with Channel 10's San Diego Leadership Award during our second youth outreach event. Kids who lived at the poverty level got to ride in limousines and paint ceramic plates with a picture demonstrating one of the "Eight Principals of Making Good Choices" that Dave and I advocate. They left with a reminder in hand to "say no" to violence and drugs.

My greatest joy came when victims called the toll-free message center or e-mailed about how relieved they were to find us. They felt less alone. I remember the day that we delivered our first personal alarm system to a victimized woman who was afraid to leave her house. A proactive organization, we scour newspaper and Internet crime reports, contact victims, and let them know that we exist and want to help.

I set up free self-defense classes for employees of crime-targeted industries to join in our movement. I knew firsthand the great benefit of working through the trauma with exercise and kickboxing; it was one of the many ways Breea and I got through our pain.

By this time, our personal healing was not the only thing happening. The Violent Trauma Awareness Project was creating a space for other victims to heal as well, lessening the trauma from being devastated by violent crime.

One night, when I was through with my work for the day, I wrote a poem that describes the release I experienced as I emerged from the most terrible kind of emotional storm:

THE THORN

My tears make way for colorful rainbows.
My pain paves the jagged way to truth.
It is so easy to see the jewels of joy.
Sewn into the beauty strewn across a sunlit dawn.
But I ask not to know only what is obvious to the
*   open eye.*
I beg on bended knee to be complete.
Knowing the value of the thorn.

I had come to consider the crime a thorn in the stem of the flower that blossomed ultimately into a new direction. I have come to learn that the thorns in life have the most value. In the end, although I believed there was a way for Breea and me to heal, I never expected that I could help others do the same thing. But once I'd found my voice, I had found my mission and I was willing to shout it at the top of my lungs. My vow was to do everything I could to spare others the trauma that nearly robbed my daughter and myself of our right to be free; mind, body, and soul.

Today, looking back, I see that my current sense of accomplishment, service, and safety was born on the worst day of my life, when all seemed lost and eternally irretrievable. Now, the comings and goings of my day-to-day life have become an extended wish for peace and service to others, making me happier, more at peace with who I am, and more fulfilled than at any other time.

I have no idea what I should do next, but I've been told that those who surrender to good works in their lives will be equipped.

I surrender.

UPDATE

B REEA is thirteen. She continues to heal from her ordeal. She reduced me to tears (never a difficult job) when she recently said, "All of my brain was messed up because of the crime, but now only a quarter of it feels messed up. It might always be that way. I remember every single detail, Mommy, and I always will. But at least they're in jail and we're free."

I couldn't be more proud that Breea made the school honor roll. She is a student council representative, a citizen of the month, and she cheers and plays sports and started an after-school club to raise money for violent crime victims, the Girls against Crime Club. She was awarded the Peace Hero Award and stood up in front of three hundred people and shared her powerful message: to never give up. But her most powerful achievement to date is that she can sleep alone in her own bed, in her own room, without nightmares.

Dave, my brother, friend, and hero, is back to

work in the communications industry. He sparkles when he describes his work with the youth program for the foundation. It's all about reaching out, he and I agree on that, and I am gratified that Dave is finally free to go about his life and to be an amazing father to my nephew Shawn, no longer burdened with worrying about my life.

Kristi continues to be the epitome of a best friend. As close as we were for those seventeen years leading up to the crime, our bond of friendship is even tighter than ever.

My mom, a survivor just like Breea and me, has joined my efforts to educate crime victims and hopes to one day share her wish for women all over the world: may they never fall into the trap of asking, "What did I do wrong that made him hit me?" My oldest sister has come back into my life after nine years of estrangement. She grew up as my mother's secret, which she now has to sort out for herself.

I showed up at her door one day and asked her to forgive me for whatever had happened. It turned into a gabfest as we reminisced for hours, catching up on life. Our first family reunion took place at her house in 2005. What a joy for all of us to see each other and revel in the growth of our family. And although we have such separate lives, the picture of most of us together that day is imbedded in my heart.

It seems that all of us, my siblings and I, are at long last sorting through the rubble of our childhoods, finding the good to hold on to and leaving the rest behind. We are all older, hopefully wiser, and just now opening up to each other about the life we led as kids. As one of my brothers, Eric, stated recently, "We went through hell, didn't we?" Yes, indeed we did. And another said, "We didn't have a chance." I say our chance is now!

The miracle of miracles is that I've had several real conversations with my dad in the past year, more than we shared in my entire lifetime. My life is all about love and forgiveness and I can finally see him in a gentler way. A man in his midsixties, he's married to a woman thirty years his junior and they have a baby boy. I watched my dad treating him tenderly and reminded him that this was his chance to do for the baby what he couldn't do for us. He nodded and called my cell phone the next day to thank me for the visit and the flowers.

I accept the fact that my dad and I will never have a solid, intimate relationship because I've stopped trying to understand him. I have learned to set boundaries, and I know that he will always believe that beating sense into his wife and children was the right thing to do. Still, seeing him in church on his birthday this year reminded me that there is always hope.

I received a call from a woman named Judy just after our story aired on Court TV. She is the foster mother of two of Lisa Ramirez's children. She told me about the call she had taken from Lisa while she was in jail. She confessed everything and had told the woman I was innocent. She said it broke her heart to read what the papers, what the defense was saying about me. She knew the truth. Judy called to thank me for testifying, for staying strong during the ordeal, and for helping to put the criminals behind bars. "Without this ever happening," she said, "these children would still be in that house with those people. This wonderful little girl might be pimped out or on drugs by now and the little boy, who knows where he would end up." I was in tears. She has since moved them out of state and legally adopted them as her own.

And me, well, I have come to realize that a person can become rich by losing everything. In fact, I can see today that when I was the most broken, I was afforded my greatest chance to become whole again, more whole than before.

My heart is with the community as I expand my outreach efforts to assist victims whose lives have been turned upside down in the aftermath of a violent crime. I am thriving in the midst of it, in spite of my past, as I trust God implicitly and keep my attention focused on truth, laughter, and love.

My greatest wish is to be an ambassador for peace. This is always on my mind as I plan the last piece of my healing. I hope to make a visit to the prison where three incarcerated men in orange jumpsuits and chains now live. I plan to capture my journey in a documentary called *Beyond Blame*™.

I can do this and I *will* do it, although as yet, I

don't know when. I've learned to turn over the timing of things to a higher power, since my own timing never seems to come out right, anyway. I only know that as my daughter and I move forward in life, we are discovering that all things are possible with the help of family, friends, and a whole lot of faith.

FACTS

I can say that with a fraction of the enormous amount of money a large financial institution spent to buy precious ad space during the Olympic Games, they could have made their employees a great deal safer. What if one of the largest sponsors of the Olympic Games refused to pay two hundred dollars a month in insurance premiums for a traumatized employee and her daughter after being targeted for a violent crime because of her job? It happened.

Crime-targeted industries should consider the amount of money that could be saved by protecting and educating employees more effectively by way of reducing the cost of retraining new employees when a victimized employee leaves, and hiring temporary staff to replace traumatized employees. That doesn't even address the ongoing trauma a victimized employee goes through, and the relapses he or she may suffer later in life, requiring them to go on leave again.

As the Olympics security staff proudly showed off

the latest hi-tech devices to ensure the safety of the athletes and their fans, I wondered why crime-targeted industries did not place the safety of their workforce and prevention on top of their "to-do" list. With the safety technologies available, why didn't financial institutions and other violent crime-targeted industries assume more of a leadership position in protecting their most valuable asset: their workforce? Is a bank manager less important than a construction worker who, by law, must be trained and warned about all the hazards he might encounter on a building site or less at risk than a hazardous materials worker, who again, by law, must receive material-specific training for the dangerous chemicals he or she might contact in their jobs?

The current social climate certainly calls for change.

DID YOU KNOW . . .

- The 2004 National Crime Report states that 18 percent of all violent crimes were work-related, and 2.4 percent of all robberies are bank robberies.

- Fifty percent of employment-related crimes involve the use of a weapon, a threat to life.

- Since 1995, bank robbery involving intimidation or kidnapping has tripled.

- Bank robbery occurs across the nation at the rate of one bank robbery every fifty-one minutes—equating to 17.5 million dollars annually lost by our financial institutions—and creating skyrocketing insurance rates. Only 20 percent is reported as recovered.

- Banks still use questionable security measures that only work when you press two buttons simultaneously. (Effective security measures, in my case, would have captured footage of Butler and Ramirez in the bank.)

- Twenty-seven percent of all bank robberies involve kidnapping or hostage-taking. There is virtually no training provided to employees in any crime-targeted industry about home invasion or post-traumatic stress disorder. (It should be mandatory.)

- Losses due to robbery are covered under an insurance plan for financial institutions and protect liquid assets. Extortion insurance is available, but rarely covers branch personnel.

- The primary victim in bank robberies is the financial institution, not the person, according to UCR, a national instant-based reporting system.

- 1.8 million people in America became violent crime victims in 2004.*

- Violent crime increased 2.5 percent in 2005.

- Post-traumatic stress disorder, or PTSD, experienced by victims of violent crime is often misdiagnosed, yet affects most victims, youth and adult, of violent crime with haunting reality. (National Center for PTSD.)

- Twenty-four thousand people become victims of violent crime during bank robberies each year, not including traumatized patrons at the scene(s).

- Many banks are not deterring robbers effectively—as the Bank Security Act of 1968 states a bank must—or training employees about the risk of home invasion robberies, which have been reported by FDIC and FBI as "on the rise" since the mid-1990s. Home invasion is not mentioned in the Bank Act of 1968.

- In 2004, there were more than a dozen kidnapping/hostage robberies across the country involving workplace employees and, in many cases, their families.

- Many teenage hotel night clerks, bank tellers, and convenience store clerks are victimized and begin their working careers with a threat-of-life incident.

- Many tellers and clerks who report being victimized are still between seventeen and nineteen.

- The majority of violent crimes committed in our country are by people ages fourteen to twenty-

four. Many are victims of violent crimes themselves.*

- There are more than 300,000 suspected criminal
  street gang members in California alone.

*Federal Bureau of Crime Statistics.

ACKNOWLEDGMENTS

B<small>Y</small> His strength and not our own, we triumphed over despair. God, you are my rock.

Without you, Breea, life would be gray. You are every color, my favorite color! "Just be brave and never give up, Mommy," are the words I cling to, still. You are my miracle. You are my angel, my joy, the greatest gift and greatest love of my life. I love you for eternity.

Dave: my brother, my friend, my hero. You showed up for us, put your own life in the background, and reminded me what family is all about when I thought all was lost and hopeless. I can't even count how many times you've said to me "You're awesome." So are you, and remember, "it's all about the summit."

Kristi: my soul friend, my sister in so many ways. Remember when I told you "I don't know how to give up"? Thank you for never giving up on me. I am so blessed to have you to travel with through life. Here's to the twin rocking chairs on that wrap-around porch we dream of.☺

Mom: I honor you for going on your own journey after this tragedy to discover your own peace of heart and mind. I am so proud of you. I love you deeply.

Mike and Jen, Ernie, sweet Shawn, Judy, Jeff, Debbie and all the other family and friends who have supported me and challenged me in so many ways, encouraging me to fight for new laws, giving of themselves to provide for outreach and awareness programs and events, so many prayers, and even making me coffee when I was barely able to keep my eyes open. All the while you allowed me to grow and learn to trust again. I love you so very much.

Ibola Kantor: You are an amazing woman, a blessing to me and to your field of trauma therapy. Without you I would not be who I am today. With all my heart I thank you.

Andrea Cagan: What a true blessing you are, and one of the brightest lights I have ever met. You have been my soul mate in this project, this gorgeous and fulfilling process. I can never thank you enough, and I cannot wait to begin our next delicious project together!

I am forever in debt to Richard and Sally Crawford for introducing me to Andrea and embracing my story, my family, and my foundation with such warmth, love, and dedication. Your integrity is so appreciated.

To Violent Trauma Awareness Project (formerly VOW) sponsors and supporters, I can't thank you enough for giving of yourself and your resources to reach out for positive change in the fight against violent crime in our society.

To the investigators, the FBI, and the prosecution team: Tony, Tom, "Taco" Rudy, Dale, Jeff, Grant, Jerry, and, of course, Diane: You all have taught me so much. I will never be able to share with you how much I appreciate all of your efforts, hard work, and the sacrifices you made in order to put these violent criminals behind bars.

To the Honorable Judge Joan Weber: Thank you for imposing maximum sentences for those convicted and announcing that Butler's version of what happened was "an outrageous pack of lies." I felt vindicated in that moment, and for that I cannot express my gratitude enough.

To all who are supportive of the Crime Victims' Integrity Bill. Your efforts will someday help so many.

To John Walsh: Thank you for taking a personal interest in our story, aiding in the capture of the final suspect, and inviting us to be on your show. You have inspired me to be a better person and to use my voice for the many who have yet to find theirs.

A gigantic thank-you to Jill Marsal, my wonderful agent with the Dijkstra Literary Agency, and Samantha Mandor, my amazing editor, who took a chance on me, for without you both this story, this message, would not have been cast out into the world to touch people's lives.

To all victims of violent crime: I give to you my daughter's words, spoken to an interviewer for a well-known book series. Breea's words continue to inspire me to heal and grow and be better than I ever dreamed

I could be: "Just because a sad and scary thing happened to me doesn't mean the rest of my life has to be sad and scary. Just be brave and never give up."

To those who didn't believe, who said I was crazy and ridiculous for even trying, those who tried to become involved in this story, in my life, for all the wrong reasons . . . thank you for intensifying my drive, thank you for the strength I gained because of you, and thank you for helping me to realize that every encounter has its purpose.

VIOLENT CRIME VICTIM AND PTSD RESOURCES

Violent Trauma Awareness Project
www.vtap.org

National Organization for Victim Assistance
www.try-nova.org

National Center for Victims of Crime
www.ncvc.org

Office for Victims of Crime
www.ojp.usdoj.gov/ovc

National Center for PTSD
www.ncptsd.va.gov

Michelle Renee is a former assistant vice president for one of the largest banks in America. Michelle has extensive experience in public speaking and community outreach. She has been recently recognized for her work in crime victims outreach and advocacy, violent offender recovery projects, and violent trauma education efforts for the San Diego District Attorney's Office, Children's Hospital Chadwick Center, and NYPD Bomb Squad, to name a few. Michelle continues her efforts across the country through the organization she founded, The Violent Trauma Awareness Project, and is striving for new legislation to protect violent crime victims in court through the Victim Integrity Bill.

Held Hostage is Michelle's first book. A second project, *Fear Fear Go Away,* a tool to assist and encourage adults and youth to work through violent trauma together, is currently in progress. Michelle and her daughter reside in Southern California.